POLITICS
& REGIMES

Editor-in-Chief
Paul Gottfried

Editor
Chris Woltermann

Editorial Board
Harold O.J. Brown
Allan C. Carlson
Jude Doherty
John Gray
Andrew Greeley
Wallace McCaffrey
Jacob Neusner
Robert Nisbet (1913–1996)
Frederick F. Ritsch
Claes G. Ryn
Gerhard Spiegler
Peter J. Stanlis

Assistant Editors
Daniel Jones
Brian Mikulski
Robert Miller
Glenn R. Neufeld
William Patch

PAUL GOTTFRIED
EDITOR

POLITICS & REGIMES

RELIGION & PUBLIC LIFE

VOLUME
30

TRANSACTION PUBLISHERS
New Brunswick (U.S.A.) and London (U.K.)

Copyright © 1997 by Transaction Publishers.
New Brunswick, New Jersey 08903.

All rights reserved under International and Pan-American Copyright Conventions. No part of this book may be reproduced or transmitted in any form or by any means, electronic or mechanical, including photocopy, recording, or any information storage and retrieval system, without prior permission in writing from the publisher. All inquiries should be addressed to Transaction Publishers, Rutgers—The State University, New Brunswick, New Jersey 08903.

This book is printed on acid-free paper that meets the American National Standard for Permanence of Paper for Printed Library Materials.

ISSN: 1083-2270
ISBN: 1-56000-908-X
Printed in the United States of America

Volumes 1 through 28 were originally published under the title *This World: An Annual of Religion and Public Life.*

Contents

The Western State as a Paradigm: Learning from History *Hans-Hermann Hoppe*	1
Epistemological Circularity as a Justification for Liberal Democracy *Aryeh Botwinick*	27
The End of the Cold War and the Collapse of Conservative and Liberal Statism *Robert J. Bresler*	40
The Vryheid Front on South Africa's Constitution *Chris Woltermann*	51
The Search for Reality: Trilling versus Parrington *James J. Novak*	57
Good Death: Is Euthanasia the Answer? *Anthony M. Matteo*	63

THE BOOKSHELF

Islam and Politics, Third Edition, by John L. Esposito reviewed by Jeremy Pizzola	76
Alexandre Kojève: The Roots of Postmodern Politics, by Shadia B. Drury reviewed by Paul Gottfried	78
The Revolt of the Elites and the Betrayal of Democracy, by Christopher Lasch reviewed by Melanie Burke Reiser	81
Redeeming America: Piety and Politics in the *New Christian Right,* by Michael Lienesch reviewed by Daniel J. Jones	84

*The Bell Curve: Intelligence and Class Structure in
American Life,* by Richard Herrnstein and Charles Murray 86
   reviewed by Alan J. Levine

Making Men Moral, by Robert P. George 92
   reviewed by Anthony M. Matteo

*Higher Superstition: The Academic Left and Its Quarrels
With Science,* by Paul R. Gross and Norman Levitt 96
   reviewed by Alan J. Levine

Contributors 99

An Editorial Note

Paul Gottfried

Volume 30 of the annual *Religion and Public Life* (formerly *This World*) centers on questions of political theory and political practice. The feature articles and book reviews both deal with these topics, and the detailed essays by Anthony Matteo, Robert Bresler, Hans-Hermann Hoppe, and Chris Woltermann examine the problem of legitimacy from differing perspectives. Basic to all our contributions is the making of political discussion both lively and philosophic, and the hesitation displayed by some of our authors to venture conclusive answers does not keep them from raising provocative questions.

The most experimental aspect of this issue was the role played by my students in putting it together. Several of them—Daniel Jones, Bill Patch, Brian Mikulski, Bob Miller, and Jeremy Pizzola—provided their services in preparing the manuscripts for publication. Some students also contributed book reviews and screened other books to determine their suitability for review. Without these services, this issue would have been long delayed and would now look less professional. Running a periodical on a shoestring does have a positive side. It brings out energies and talent that those recruited for editorial tasks would not otherwise learn that they possessed. In any case I am grateful to those raw recruits who shaped up under fire. Without them, their commander would still be clueless in the trenches. It would also be an oversight not to express gratitude to Elizabethtown College and Transaction Publishers. Both have shown faith in our enterprise and furnished the wherewithal to keep it going. That this annual is now attracting widespread attention from, among others, the Episcopal Arch-Bishop of New York is clear proof that their faith was not misplaced.

The Western State as a Paradigm: Learning from History

Hans–Hermann Hoppe

If one decides to write on what to learn from the history of Western states, one must be convinced that there *is* something to be learned; and if one holds this to be the case, then one must reject two alternative views: the so–called Whig theory of history and historicism.[1]

According to the Whig theory of history, mankind marches continuously forward. Human history is the record of progress. Better ideas replace worse ones; still better ideas come along later; and so on, forever. If this is the case, nothing can be learned from history. All one can do is first identify the most progressive society and then imitate its rules and institutions. Pursuant to the Whig theory, the people of Eastern Europe and the Third World can do no better than to imitate the Western European and U.S. democratic welfare states. There is no need for anyone to study the distant past because, *by assumption,* no mistakes have ever occurred in history. Whatever happened later was an improvement on what occurred earlier; hence, there is never any reason to study anything but the most progressive society's recent past, the most progressive of all ages.

According to historicism, there is no such thing as a moral "right" or "wrong," and all ethical judgements are subjective. Moreover, with the possible exception of the laws of logic, mathematics, and the natural sciences, no universal positive laws exist. Economics and sociology are only history, a chronicle of past actions and events, with no more to be learned from it than that "this is the way it was."

Both of these views, the Whig theory of history and historicism, are unacceptable. In their stead, I assume that both ethical truths and nonhypothetically true positive laws of economics and sociology exist. These assumptions make it possible to identify some fundamentally wrong turns in the history of the Western state.

---

[1] See also R. Nisbet, *History of the Idea of Progress* (New York: Basic Books, 1980); L. v. Mises, *Theory and History* (Auburn: Ludwig von Mises Institute, 1985); M. N. Rothbard, *Economic Thought Before Adam Smith. An Austrian Perspective on the History of Economic Thought* 1 (Albershot: Edward Elgar, 1995); idem, *Classical Economics. An Austrian Perspective on the History of Economic Thought* 2 (Aldershot: Edward Elgar 1995).

Lesson One: Against Centralization

A state is a territorial monopolist of force. It is an agency that may engage in continual, institutionalized property rights violations and the exploitation—through expropriation, taxation, and regulation—of private property owners.[2] Assuming no more than self-interest on the part of governmental agents, every state (government) can be expected to make use of its monopoly and thus exhibit a tendency toward *increased* exploitation. On the one hand, this means increased internal exploitation (and not only via taxation); on the other hand, it means territorial expansion. States will always try to enlarge their opportunities for exploitation. In doing so, they will come into conflict with other, competing states. The competition between states, *qua* territorial monopolists of compulsion, is by its very nature an eliminative contest. That is, there can only be one monopolist of exploitation in any given area; thus, competition between states can be expected to promote a tendency toward increased political centralization and ultimately one, single, world state.

A glance at Western history suffices to illustrate the validity of this conclusion. At the beginning of this millennium, for instance, Europe consisted of thousands of independent political units. Now, only several dozen such units remain. To be sure, decentralizing forces also operated. There was the progressive disintegration of the Ottoman Empire from the sixteenth century until after World War I and the establishment of modern Turkey. The ethnically heterogeneous Habsburg Empire was gradually dismembered from the time of its greatest expansion under Charles V, until it disappeared and modern Austria was founded in 1918. And only recently, before our very eyes, the former Soviet Empire disintegrated. However, the overriding tendency has been in the opposite direction. For instance, during the second half of the seventeenth century, German consisted of some 234 countries, 51 free cities, and 1,500 independent knightly manors. By the early nineteenth century, the total number of the three had fallen to below 50, and by 1871 unification had been achieved. The scenario in Italy was similar. Even small states have a history of expansion and centralization. Switzerland began in 1291 as a confederation of three independent cantonal states. By 1848, it was a single (federal) state with some two dozen cantonal provinces.

Moreover, from a global perspective, mankind has come closer than ever before to the establishment of a world government. Even before the dissolution of the Soviet Union, the United States had attained hegemonic status over Western Europe (most notably West Germany) and the Pacific rim countries (most notably Japan). Several indications of the U.S. position are: the presence of American troops and military bases; the NATO and SEATO pacts; the roles of the American dollar as the ultimate international reserve currency and of the U.S. Federal Reserve System as the "liquidity provider" of last resort for the entire Western banking system; and American-dominated institutions such as the International Monetary Fund (IMF), the World Bank, and the recently established World Trade Organization (WTO). In addition,

---

[2] On the theory of the state, see M. N. Rothbard, *For A New Liberty* (New York: Macmillan, 1978); idem, *The Ethics of Liberty* (Atlantic Highlands, N.J: Humanities Press, 1982); idem, *Power and Market* (Kansas City, Kans.: Sheed, Andrews, and McMeel, 1977); H. H. Hoppe, *Eigentum, Anarchie und Staat* (Opladen: Westdeutscher Verlag, 1987); idem, *A Theory of Socialism and Capitalism* (Boston: Kluwer, 1989); idem, *The Economics and Ethics of Private Property* (Boston: Kluwer, 1993); also A. J. Nock, *Our Enemy the State* (Delevan: Hallberg Publishing, 1983); F. Oppenheimer, *The State* (New York: Vanguard Press, 1914); idem, *System der Soziologie* 2: Der Staat (Stuttgart: G. Fischer, 1964).

American hegemony has steadily fostered the political integration of Western Europe. With the establishment of a European Central Bank and a European Currency Unit (ECU), the European Community will likely be complete before the turn of the century. At the same time, with the North American Free Trade Agreement (NAFTA), a significant step toward the political integration of the American continent has been taken. In the absence of the Soviet Empire and its military threat, the U.S. has emerged as the world's sole and undisputed military superpower and its "top cop."

According to the orthodox view, centralization is generally a "good" and progressive movement, whereas disintegration and secession, even if sometimes unavoidable, are anachronistic. It is assumed that larger political units—and, ultimately, a single world government—imply wider markets and, hence, increased wealth. Putative evidence for this is that economic prosperity has increased dramatically in the wake of centralization. However, rather than reflecting any truth, this orthodox view is more illustrative of the fact that history is typically written by its victors. Neither correlation nor temporal coincidence proves causation. In fact, the relationship between economic prosperity and centralization is very different from and, indeed, almost the opposite of what orthodoxy alleges.[3]

Political integration (centralization) and economic (market) integration are two completely different phenomena. Political integration involves the territorial expansion of a state's power of taxation and property regulation. Economic integration is the extension of the interpersonal and interregional division of labor and market participation. In principle, in taxing and regulating private property owners and market income earners, all governments are counterproductive. They *reduce* market participation and the formation of wealth. Once the existence of a government has been assumed, however, no direct relationship between territorial size and economic integration exists. Centralization can go hand in hand with either economic progress or retrogression. Progress results whenever a less taxing and regulating government expands its territory at the expense of a more exploitative one. If the reverse occurs, centralization implies economic disintegration and retrogression.

Yet, a highly important indirect relationship exists between size and economic integration. A central government ruling over large-scale territories cannot come into existence *ab ovo*. Instead, all institutions with the power to tax and regulate owners of private property must start out small. Smallness contributes to moderation, however. A small government has many close competitors, and if it taxes and regulates its subjects visibly more than its competitors do theirs, it is bound to suffer from the emigration of labor and capital and a corresponding loss of future tax revenue.[4]

---

[3] On the political economy of centralization and decentralization, see also J. Baechler, *The Origins of Capitalism* (New York: St. Martin's, 1976), esp. chap. 7; H. H. Hoppe, "Against Centralization," *Salisbury Review* (June 1993); idem, "Migrazione, centralismo e secessione nell'Europa contemporanea," *biblioteca della liberta* no. 118 (1992).

[4] Political competition is a far more effective device for limiting a government's natural desire to expand its exploitative powers than are internal constitutional limitations. Indeed, the attempts of some public choice theorists and of "constitutional economics" to design model liberal constitutions must strike one as hopelessly naive. For constitutional courts are part and parcel of the government apparatus whose powers they are supposed to limit. Why in the world should they want to constrain the power of the very organization that provides them with jobs, money, and prestige? To assume so is theoretically inconsistent, that is, incompatible with the assumption of self-interest. The naive constitutional approach is equally without historical foundation. Despite the explicit limitation of the power of the central government contained in the Tenth Amendment of the U.S. Constitution, the U.S. Supreme Court has rendered the amendment essentially null and void.

Contrary to orthodoxy, then, it is precisely the fact that Europe possessed a highly decentralized power structure composed of numerous independent political units that explains the origin of capitalism in the Western world. It is not by accident that capitalism first flourished under conditions of extreme political decentralization: in the northern Italian city states, in southern Germany, and in the secessionist Low Countries (Netherlands).

The competition among small states for taxable subjects brings them into conflict with each other. As a result of interstate conflicts, drawn out over the course of centuries, a few states succeed in expanding their territories, while others are eliminated or incorporated. Which states win in this process depends on many factors, but, in the long run, the decisive factor is the relative amount of economic resources at a government's disposal. In taxing and regulating, governments do not positively contribute to the creation of economic wealth. Instead, they parasitically draw on existing wealth. However, they can influence the amount of existing wealth negatively.

Other things being equal, the lower the tax and regulation burden imposed by a government on its domestic economy, the larger its population tends to grow (due to internal reasons as well as immigration), and the larger the amount of domestically produced wealth on which it can draw in its conflicts with neighboring competitors. For this reason, centralization is frequently progressive. Liberal states that tax and regulate their domestic economies little tend to defeat and expand their territories at the expense of nonliberal ones. This accounts for the outbreak of the Industrial Revolution in centralized England and France. It explains why, in the course of the nineteenth century, Western Europe came to dominate the rest of the world, and why this colonialism was generally progressive. Furthermore, it explains the rise of the U.S. to the rank of superpower in the course of the twentieth century.

However, the further the process of more liberal governments defeating less liberal ones proceeds—that is, the larger the territories, the fewer and more distant the remaining competitors, and the more costly international migration—the lower becomes a government's incentive to continue its domestic liberalism. As one approaches the limit of a One World state, all possibilities of voting with one's feet against a government disappear. Wherever one goes, the same tax and regulation structure applies. Relief from the threat of emigration removes a fundamental rein on the expansion of governmental power. This explains developments of the twentieth century: with World War I, and even more so with World War II, the U.S. attained hegemony over Western Europe and became heir to its vast colonial empires. A decisive step in the direction of global unification was taken with the establishment of a *pax Americana*. Indeed, throughout the entire period, the U.S., Western Europe, and most of the rest of the world have suffered from a steady and dramatic growth of government power, taxation, and regulatory expropriation.[5]

In light of social and economic theory and history, then, a first lesson follows: a plea for secession. Initially, secession is nothing more than a shifting of control over nationalized wealth from a larger, central government to a smaller, regional one. Whether this will lead to more or less economic integration and prosperity depends largely on the new regional government's policies. However, the sole fact of secession has a positive impact on production insofar as it reduces or eliminates "forced integration."

---

[5] On this theme, see P. Johnson, *Modern Times* (New York: Harper & Row, 1983); R. Nisbet, *The Present Age* (New York: Harper & Row, 1988).

As a result of centuries of centralization, hundreds of distinct cultures have been extirpated. The process of centralization has also led to the economic exploitation and cultural domination of one ethnic, linguistic, religious, or cultural group by another, for example, of the Irish, Scots, and Welsh by the English; the Slovenes and Croats by the Serbs; and the Estonians, Lithuanians, and Latvians by the Russians. Forced integration, as illustrated by measures such as busing, affirmative action, and antidiscrimination laws, invariably creates tension, hatred, and conflict. In contrast, voluntary separation leads to social harmony and peace. Under forced integration, any mistake can be blamed on a "foreign" group or culture and all success claimed as one's own; hence, there is little or no reason for any culture to learn from another. Under a regime of "separate but equal," one must face up to the realities of cultural diversity and of visibly different ranks of cultural advancement. If a secessionist people wishes to improve or maintain its position vis-à-vis a competing one, nothing but discriminative learning will help. It must imitate, assimilate, and, if possible, improve upon the skills, traits, practices, and rules characteristic of more advanced cultures, and it must avoid those characteristic of less advanced societies. Rather than promoting a downward leveling of cultures as under forced integration, secession stimulates a cooperative process of cultural selection and advancement.

In particular, secession can also eliminate the immigration problem increasingly plaguing the countries of Western Europe as well as the U.S. Now, whenever a central government permits immigration, it allows foreigners to proceed—literally on government–owned roads—to any of its residents' doorsteps, regardless of whether these residents desire such proximity to foreigners. "Free immigration" is, to a large extent, forced integration. Secession solves this problem by letting smaller territories have their own admission standards to determine independently with whom they will associate at close range and with whom they prefer to cooperate from a distance.[6]

Moreover, while everything else depends on the new regional government's domestic policies and no direct relationship between size and economic integration exists, there is an important indirect connection. Just as political centralization ultimately tends to promote economic disintegration, so secession tends to advance integration and economic development. Secession always involves increased opportunities for interregional migration, so a secessionist government is immediately confronted with the specter of emigration. To avoid the loss of its most productive subjects, it comes under increased pressure to adopt comparatively liberal domestic policies by allowing more private property and imposing a lower tax and regulation burden than its neighbors. Ultimately, with as many territories as separate households, villages, or towns, the opportunities for economically motivated emigration is maximized, and government power over a domestic economy minimized.

Moreover, the smaller the country, the greater will be the pressure to opt for free trade rather than protectionism. All government interference with foreign trade forcibly limits the range of mutually beneficial interterritorial exchanges and thus leads to relative impoverishment, at home as well as abroad. But the smaller a territory and its internal markets, the more dramatic this effect will be. A country the size of the U.S., for instance, might attain comparatively high standards of living even if it renounced

---

[6] On the problem of immigration, see M. N. Rothbard, "Nations by Consent: Decomposing the Nation–State," *Journal of Libertarian Studies* 11, no. 1 (1994); H. H. Hoppe, "Free Immigration or Forced Integration?" *Chronicles* (June 1995).

all foreign trade, provided it possessed an unrestricted internal capital and consumer goods market. In contrast, consider a single household as the conceivably smallest secessionist unit. By engaging in unrestricted free trade, even the smallest territory can be fully integrated into the world market and partake of every advantage of the division of labor; its owners could well become the wealthiest people on earth. The existence of a single wealthy individual anywhere is living proof of this. On the other hand, if the same household owners were to forego all interterritorial trade, abject poverty or death would result. Accordingly, the smaller a territory and its internal markets, the more likely it is that it will opt for free trade.

Secession also promotes *monetary* integration. The process of centralization has resulted in the formation of an international cartel, dominated by the American government, of managed trade and migration, ever more invasive and burdensome governments, globalized welfare–warfare statism, and stagnant or even declining standards of living. It has also resulted in monetary disintegration: the destruction of the former international commodity (gold) money standard and its replacement with a dollar–dominated system of freely fluctuating government paper monies, that is, a global, U.S.–led, governmental counterfeiting cartel. This system of freely fluctuating paper currencies is no monetary system at all.[7] It is a system of partial *barter*; it is detrimental to the purpose of money, to facilitate exchange. This becomes obvious once it is recognized that there is no special economic significance attached to the way national borders are drawn. And, if one imagines a proliferation of ever smaller national territories, ultimately to the point where each household forms its own country, fiat paper currency stands revealed for the outright absurdity it is. For if every household were to issue its own paper currency, the world would be right back at barter. No one would accept anyone else's paper, economic calculation would be impossible, and trade would come to a virtual standstill. From this theoretical insight it follows that secession, provided it proceeds far enough, will actually promote monetary integration. In a world of hundreds of thousands of Monacos, Andorras, San Marinos, Liechtenstein, Singapores, and Hong Kongs, each country would have to abandon fiat money, which has been responsible for the greatest global inflation in human history, and once again adopt an international commodity money system such as the gold standard.

Lesson Two: Against Democratization

Besides the tendency toward political centralization, the history of the Western states, and indeed of all states, has been characterized by another fundamental structural change: the transition from monarchical to democratic rule. In accordance with the rule that history is typically written by its victors, this change, too, is generally presented as a progressive development. However, in light of elementary economic theory, this interpretation also turns out to be largely unfounded, and the tendency toward democratization must indeed be interpreted as *reinforcing* the tendency toward increased exploitation caused by political centralization.[8]

---

[7] See M. N. Rothbard, *The Case for a 100 Percent Gold Dollar* (Auburn: Ludwig von Mises Institute, 1991); idem, *The Case Against the Fed* (Auburn: Ludwig von Mises Institute, 1995); H. H. Hoppe, "How is Fiat Money Possible?—or, The Devolution of Money and Credit," *Review of Austrian Economics* 7, no. 2 (1994).

[8] On the following, see H. H. Hoppe, "Time Preference, Government, and the Process of De–Civilization. From Monarchy to Democracy," *Journal des Economistes et des Etudes Humaines* 5, no. 4 (1994).

For most of its history, mankind, insofar as it was subject to any government control at all, was under monarchical rule. There were exceptions: Athenian democracy, Rome during its republican era until 31 B.C., the republics of Venice, Florence, and Genoa during the Renaissance period, the Swiss cantons since 1291, the United Provinces from 1648 until 1673, and England under Cromwell from 1649 until 1660. These were, however, rare occurrences in a world dominated by monarchies. With the exception of Switzerland, they were short–lived phenomena; and, constrained by monarchical surroundings, all older republics satisfied the open–entry requirement of modern democracies only imperfectly. That is, suffrage and the right to exercise government functions were restricted to extremely small numbers of "nobles." In Athens, for instance, only 15,000 to 20,000 people, out of a population of more than 400,000, possessed the right to vote and participate in government.

The transition from monarchy to democracy did not begin until the French Revolution, and it was only at the end of World War I that mankind truly left the monarchical age. The first assault of republicanism and the idea of popular sovereignty on the dominating monarchical principle was repelled with the military defeat of Napoleon and the restoration of Bourbon rule in France. However, the democratic–republican spirit of the French Revolution left a permanent imprint. From the restoration of the monarchical order in 1815 until the outbreak of World War I in 1914, all across Europe popular political participation and representation was systematically expanded. The franchise was successively widened everywhere, and the powers of popularly elected parliaments were gradually increased.

Although increasingly emasculated, the monarchical principle remained dominant until the cataclysmic events of World War I. Before the war, only two republics existed in Europe: Switzerland and France. And, of all major European monarchies, only the United Kingdom could be classified as a parliamentary system, that is, one where the supreme power was vested in an elected parliament. Only four years later, after the U.S.—where the democratic principle had triumphed with the destruction of the secessionist Confederacy by the centralist Union government—had entered the European war and decisively determined its outcome, monarchies had all but disappeared, and Europeans had turned to democratic republicanism.[9]

In Europe, the defeated Romanovs, Hohenzollerns, and Habsburgs had to abdicate or resign, and Russia, Germany, and Austria became democratic republics with universal adult suffrage and parliamentary governments. Likewise, all of the newly created successor states—Poland, Finland, Estonia, Latvia, Lithuania, Hungary, and Czechoslovakia (with the sole exception of Yugoslavia)—adopted democratic republican constitutions. In Turkey and Greece, the monarchies were overthrown. Even where monarchies remained nominally existent, as in Great Britain, Italy, Spain, Belgium, the Netherlands, and the Scandinavian countries, monarchs no longer exercised any governing power. Universal adult suffrage was introduced, and all government power was invested in parliaments and "public" officials. The democratic–republican age, a new world order under the aegis of a dominating U.S. government, had begun.

---

[9] See G. Ferrero, *Peace and War* (Freeport: Books for Libraries Press, 1969), chap. 3; idem, *Macht* (Bern: A. Francke, 1944); B. de Jouvenel, *On Power* (New York: Viking, 1949); E. v. Kuehnelt-Leddihn, *Leftism Revisited* (Washington D.C.: H. Regnery, 1990); R. Bendix, *Kings or People* (Berkeley: University of California Press, 1978); R. R. Palmer and J. Colton, *A History of the Modern World* (New York: A. Knopf, 1992), esp. chaps. XIV, XVIII.

Interestingly, neither the proponents of democracy nor, more surprisingly, the defenders of the *ancien régime* recognized the fundamental *economic* implications of this change. From the point of view of economics, the transition from monarchy to democracy was essentially a change from a system of privately owned government to one of "publicly" owned government. Elementary economic theory leads one to suspect that the conduct of government and the effects of government policy on civil society will differ systematically depending on whether the government apparatus is owned privately or publicly.[10]

The defining characteristic of private government ownership, as exemplified by a monarchy, is that the expropriated resources and the monopoly privilege of future expropriation are individually *owned*. The appropriated resources are added to the ruler's private estate and treated as if they were a part of it, and the monopoly privilege of future expropriation is attached as a title to this estate and leads to an instant increase in its present value. Most importantly, as private owner of the government estate, the ruler is entitled to pass his possessions on to his personal heir, and he may personally employ or dismiss every administrator and employee of his estate.

In contrast, with a publicly owned government, as exemplified by a democracy, the control over the government apparatus lies in the hands of a trustee or caretaker. The caretaker may use the apparatus to his personal advantage, but he does not own it. He cannot sell government resources and privately pocket the receipts, nor can he pass government possessions on to his personal heir. He owns the *current use* of government resources, but not their capital value. Moreover, while entrance into the position of a private owner of government is restricted by the owner's personal discretion, entrance into the position of a caretaker–ruler is open. Anyone, in principle, can became the government's caretaker.

From this, two interrelated predictions can be made. First, a private government owner will tend to have a systematically longer planning horizon, that is, his degree of time preference will be lower. Accordingly, his degree of economic exploitation will tend to be less than that of a government caretaker. Second, subject to a higher degree of exploitation, the nongovernmental public will also be comparatively more present–oriented under a system of publicly owned government than under a regime of private government ownership.[11]

A private government owner will try to maximize his total wealth (the present value of his estate *and* his current income). He will *not* want to increase his current income at the expense of a more than proportional drop in the present value of his assets, and, since acts of current income acquisition invariably have repercussions on present asset values (reflecting the value of all anticipated asset earnings discounted by the rate of time preference), private ownership in and of itself leads to economic calculation and promotes farsightedness. This implies a distinct moderation with respect to the ruler's incentive to exploit his monopoly privilege of expropriation, for acts of expropriation are, by their very nature, parasitic upon prior

---

[10] See Rothbard, *Power and Market,* chap. 5; G. Hardin and J. Baden, eds., *Managing the Commons* (San Francisco: W. H. Freeman, 1977).

[11] On the theory of time preference, see in particular L. v. Mises, *Human Action* (Chicago: H. Regnery, 1966), chaps. XVIII, XIX; also W. St. Jevons, *Theory of Political Economy* (New York: A. Kelley, 1965); E. v. Boehm–Bawerk, *Capital and Interest* (South Holland: Libertarian Press, 1959); F. Fetter, *Capital Interest, and Rent* (Kansas City, Kans.: Sheed, Andrews, and McMeel, 1977); M. N. Rothbard, *Man, Economy, and State* (Los Angeles: Nash, 1970), chaps. 5–7.

acts of production on the part of the nongovernmental public. Accordingly, a private government owner will want to avoid exploiting his subjects so heavily that he reduces his future earnings potential to such an extent that the present value of his estate (the country) actually falls. He will, of course, use his monopolistic privilege; he will not *not* exploit. As the government's private owner, he realizes that it may be in his interest to draw moderately from a growing, increasingly productive and prosperous economy.

Private ownership of government implies moderation and farsightedness for yet another reason. All private property is, by definition, exclusive property. He who owns property is entitled to exclude everyone else from its use and enjoyment. Only the king and, to a minor extent, his friends, employees, and business partners share in the enjoyment of expropriated resources and can thus lead a parasitic life. Because of these restrictions regarding entrance into government, private government ownership stimulates the development of a clear class consciousness on the part of the nongovernmental public and promotes opposition and resistance to any expansion of the government's exploitative power. There being an almost insurmountable barrier to upward mobility, solidarity among the ruled is strengthened, and the risk to the king of losing his legitimacy as the result of increased exploitation is heightened.

In distinct contrast, the caretaker of a publicly owned government will not try to maximize total government wealth (capital values and current income), but will rather raise current income (regardless, and at the expense, of capital values). Instead of maintaining or even enhancing the value of the government estate, its temporary caretaker will quickly use up as much of its resources as possible, for what he does not consume *now*, he may *never* be able to consume. A caretaker, as distinct from a king, has no interest in maintaining his country. For why should he *not* want to increase his exploitation, if the advantage of a policy of moderation cannot be reaped privately, while the advantage of the opposite policy of increased exploitation can be so reaped? To a caretaker, unlike to a private owner, moderation has only disadvantages and no advantages.

With a publicly owned government, anyone can aspire to become a member of the ruling class or even the supreme power. The distinction between the rulers and the ruled as well as the class consciousness of the ruled become blurred. The illusion even arises that the distinction no longer exists, that no one is ruled by anyone while everyone rules himself. Accordingly, public resistance against government power is systematically weakened. While exploitation before might have appeared plainly oppressive to the public, it seems much less so once anyone may freely enter the ranks of those who are at the receiving end.

Regarding the effect of government conduct on civil society, governmental violations of private property rights, whether in the form of taxation, inflation (counterfeiting), or regulation, have a twofold impact on individual time preferences. On the one hand, like crime, all government interference with private property rights reduce someone else's supply of present goods and thus raises his effective time preference rate. One the other hand, government offenses, unlike crime, simultaneously raise the time preference *degree* of actual and potential victims because they also imply a reduction in the supply of *future* goods (a reduced rate of return on investment). Because governmental property rights violations are continual, the actual and potential victims respond by associating a permanently higher risk with all future production and systematically adjusting their expectations concerning the rate of return on all future investment downward. Therefore, by simultaneously reducing the supply of present *and* expected future goods, governmental property rights violations not only raise time preference *rates* (with given schedules) but also time preferences *schedules*. Because private owner–producers are, and see themselves as, defenseless against future victimization by government agents, their expected rate of return on productive, future–oriented actions is uniformly reduced; accordingly, all actual and potential victims tend to become more present–oriented.[12] Furthermore, because the degree of exploitation is comparatively higher under a publicly owned government, this tendency toward present orientation will be significantly more pronounced than if government were privately owned.

In light of these theoretical considerations, the end of World War I can be identified as the point in time at which private government ownership was completely replaced by public government ownership, and whence a systematic tendency toward increased governmental exploitation and rising degrees of social present–orientedness could be expected to take off. Indeed, such has been the grand, underlying theme of Western history since 1918.

Regarding indicators of exploitation, there is no doubt that the taxes imposed on civil society increased during the monarchical age. However, throughout the entire period, the share of government revenue remained remarkably low. Economic historian Carlo M. Cipolla observes that "it is difficult to imagine that, apart from particular time and places [such as wars], the public power ever managed to draw more than 5 to 8 percent of national product." He goes on to note that this portion was not systematically exceeded until the second half of the nineteenth century.[13] Even at the outbreak of World War I, total government expenditure as a percentage of Gross Domestic Product (GDP) typically had not risen above 10 percent and only rarely, as in the case of Germany, exceeded 15 percent. In striking contrast, with the onset of the democratic–republican age, total government expenditure as a percentage of GDP typically increased to between 20 and 30 percent in the course of the 1920s and 1930s, and, by the mid–1970s, had generally reached 50 percent.[14] Although total government employment increased during the monarchical age, until the very end of the nineteenth century, it rarely exceeded 3 percent of the total labor force. In contrast, by the mid–1970s, government employment as a percentage of the total labor force had typically gown to close to 20 percent.[15]

The same pattern emerges from an examination of inflation and data on the money supply. The monarchical world was generally characterized by the existence of a commodity money, typically gold or silver. A commodity money standard makes it difficult, if not impossible, for a government to inflate the money supply; and monarchical rulers, hard as they tried, did not succeed in establishing lasting monopolies of pure fiat currencies, that is, of irredeemable government paper monies. Accordingly, during the monarchical age the "level" of prices generally fell and the purchasing

---

[12] See Rothbard, *Power and Market,* chap. 4; A. T. Smith, *Time and Public Policy* (Knoxville: University of Tennessee Press, 1988); Hoppe, "Time Preference, Government, and the Process of De–Civilization. From Monarchy to Democracy."

[13] C. M. Cipolla, *Before the Industrial Revolution. European Society and Economy, 1000–1700* (New York: W.W. Norton, 1980), 48.

[14] See P. Flora, *State, Economy and Society in Western Europe* 1 (Campus: Frankfurt, 1983): 258–59.

[15] Flora, *State, Economy and Society in Western Europe*, chap. 8.

power of money increased, except during times of war or new gold discoveries. Various price indices for Britain, for instance, indicate that prices were substantially lower in 1760 than they had been a hundred years earlier; they were still lower in 1860 than they had been in 1760. Similarly, during the more than seventy years between 1845 and the end of World War I, the British money supply increased only about sixfold. Connected by an international gold standard, the development in other countries was similar.[16]

After 1918, under conditions of democratic republicanism, the gold standard was first replaced by a spurious gold standard, the so-called gold exchange standard, which survived until 1971. Since then, for the first time in history, the entire world has adopted a pure fiat money system of freely fluctuating government paper currencies. Accordingly, rather than a gradual increase in the purchasing power of money, a seemingly permanent secular tendency toward inflation and currency depreciation has come into existence.[17] The "level" of prices has practically always moved upward, especially since 1971, and, in the more than seventy years since 1918, the U.S. money supply, in a development with parallels throughout the world, has increased more than sixtyfold.[18]

In addition to taxation and inflation (counterfeiting), a government can resort to debt in order to finance its current expenditures. As predicted by theory, kings were more moderate borrowers than were democratic–republican caretakers. Throughout the monarchical age, government debts were essentially war debts, and, while the total debt tended to increase over time, monarchs typically reduced their debts during peacetime. In striking contrast, since the beginning of the democratic–republican age, government debts typically increased in war *and* in peace, and, since the fateful events of 1971 when a pure fiat money regime facilitating the monetization of government debt came into being, they have literally skyrocketed.[19]

The same tendency toward increased exploitation also becomes apparent from examining government legislation and regulation. During the monarchical age, with a clear–cut distinction between the ruler and the ruled, the king and his parliament were held to be *under* the law.[20] They applied preexisting law as judge or jury. They did not make law. To be sure, due to the king's monopoly of administering the law, the price of law increased and its quality decreased. But as late as the beginning of the twenti-

---

[16] See B. R. Mitchell, *Abstract of British Historical Statistics* (Cambridge: Cambridge University Press, 1962), 468ff; idem, *European Historical Statistics 1750–1970* (New York: Columbia University Press, 1978), 388ff.

[17] See M. N. Rothbard, *What Has Government Done to Our Money* (Auburn: Ludwig von Mises Institute, 1990); idem, *The Mystery of Banking* (New York: Richardson & Snyder, 1983); idem, *The Case Against the Fed*; R. Paul and L. Lehrmann, *The Case for Gold: A Minority Report to the U.S. Gold Commission* (Washington, D.C.: Cato Institute, 1982).

[18] See M. Friedman and A. Schwartz, *A Monetary History of the United States, 1867–1960* (Princeton: Princeton University Press, 1963), 702–22; *Economic Report of the President* (Washington D.C.: Government Printing Office, 1992).

[19] See S. Homer and R. Sylla, *A History of Interest Rates* (New Brunswick, N.J.: Rutgers University Press, 1991), 188, 437; J. Hughes, *American Economic History* (Glenview: Scott, Forseman, 1990), 432, 498, 589.

[20] See B. de Jouvenel, *Sovereignty* (Chicago: University of Chicago Press, 1957); also F. Kern, *Kingship and Law in the Middle Ages* (Greenwich and New York: Greeenwoood Press, 1985); B. Rehfeld, *Die Wurzeln des Rechts* (Berlin, 1951).

eth century, A. V. Dicey could still maintain that in Great Britain legislated law, as distinct from pre–existing law, did not exist.[21]

In striking contrast, under democracy, with the exercise of power shrouded in anonymity, presidents and parliaments quickly came to rise *above* the law. They became not only judge but legislator, the creator of "new" law.[22] In a development similar to the democratization of money, the democratization of law and law administration has led to a steadily growing flood of legislation. Presently, the number of legislative acts and regulations passed by parliaments in the course of a single year is in the tens of thousands, filling hundreds of thousands of pages, affecting all aspects of civil and commercial life, and resulting in a steady depreciation of all law and heightened legal uncertainty. As a typical example, the 1994 edition of the *Code of Federal Regulations,* the annual compendium of all U.S. Federal Government regulations currently in effect, consists of a total of 201 books, occupying about 26 feet of library shelf space. The Code's index alone is 754 pages.[23]

Regarding indicators of rising social time preference (present orientedness), history reveals an equally clear pattern. The most direct indicator of social time preference is the rate of interest. The interest rate is the ratio of the valuation of present goods as compared to future goods. A high interest rate implies more "present orientedness" and a low rate of interest implies more of a "future orientation." Under normal conditions, that is, under the assumption of increasing standards of living and real–money incomes, the interest rate can be expected to fall and ultimately approach, yet never quite reach, zero, for with rising real incomes, the marginal utility of present money falls relative to that of future money. Hence under the *ceteris paribus* assumption of a given time preference schedule, the interest rate must fall.

In fact, a tendency toward falling interest rates characterizes mankind's suprasecular trend of development. In thirteenth–century Europe, the lowest interest rate on "safe" long–term loans was 8 percent. In the fourteenth century, rates came down to about 5 percent. In the fifteenth century, they fell to 4 percent. In the seventeenth century they went down to 3 percent. And at the end of the nineteenth century, minimum interest rates had further declined to less than 2.5 percent.[24] This trend was by no means smooth. It was frequently interrupted, during times of wars and revolutions, by periods of rising interest rates. But the overriding tendency toward lower interest rates reflects mankind's overall advance from barbarism to civilization. Against this historical backdrop and in accordance with economic theory, it should be expected that twentieth–century interest rates would have to be still lower then nineteenth–century rates. Only two possible explanations exist why this should not be the case. The first possibility is that twentieth–century real incomes did not exceed nineteenth–century income. This explanation can be safely ruled out on empirical grounds. Only the second explanation remains. If real incomes are in fact higher but interest rates are not lower, then the *ceteris paribus* clause can no longer be assumed true. Rather,

---

[21] See A. V. Dicey, *Lectures on the Relation between Law and Public Opinion in England during the Nineteenth Century* (London: Macmillan, 1903); also F. A. Hayek, *Law Legislation, and Liberty* 1 (Chicago: University of Chicago Press, 1973), chaps. 4 and 6; B. Leoni, *Freedom and the Law* (Indianapolis, Ind.: Liberty Fund, 1991).

[22] See also R. Nisbet, *Community and Power* (New York: Oxford University Press, 1962), chap. 5.

[23] See D. Boudreaux, "The World's Biggest Government," *Free Market* (November 1994).

[24] See Homer and Sylla, *History of Interest Rates,* 557–58.

the time preference schedule must have shifted upward, that is, people on the average must have become more present oriented, which appears to be the case.

An inspection of the lowest decennial average interest rates for the Western world shows that interest rates during the entire post–World War I era were never as low or lower than they had been during the second half of the nineteenth century. This conclusion does not change, even if one takes into account that modern interest rates, in particular since the 1970s, include a systematic inflation premium. After adjusting recent nominal interest rates for inflation in order to yield an estimate of real interest rates, contemporary rates still appear to be significantly higher than those of 100 years ago. On the average, minimum long–term interest rates in Europe and the U.S. nowadays seem to be well above 4 percent, and possibly as high as 5 percent, or above the interest rates of seventeenth–century Europe and as high or higher than fifteenth–century rates.[25]

Parallel to this development and reflecting a more specific aspect of the same underlying phenomenon of high or rising social time preferences, indicators of family disintegration have exhibited a systematic increase. Until the end of the nineteenth century, the bulk of government spending went into financing the military. Welfare spending played almost no role. Insurance was considered to be in the province of individual responsibility, and poverty relief was seen as the task of voluntary charity. In contrast, as a reflection of the egalitarianism inherent in democracy, the late nineteenth century saw the beginning of the collectivization of individual responsibility. This has proceeded so far that the bulk of public spending nowadays is eaten up by welfare expenditures: by compulsory government "insurance" against illness, occupational injuries, old age, unemployment, and an ever-expanding list of other "disabilities."[26] Consequently, by increasingly relieving individuals of the responsibility of having to provide for their own health, safety, and old age, the range and the temporal horizon of private provisionary action have been systematically reduced. In particular, the value of marriage, family, and children have fallen because they are less needed when one can fall back on "public" assistance. Since the onset of the democratic–republican age, the birth rate in Western countries fell from 30 to 40 per 1,000 population to about 15 to 20.[27] At the same time, the rates of divorce, illegitimacy, single parenting, singledom, and abortion have steadily increased, while personal savings rates have begun to stagnate or even fall rather than rise proportional or over–proportional to rising incomes.[28]

Moreover, as a consequence of the depreciation of law resulting from an unabating flood of legislation and the collectivization of responsibility effected by welfare policies, the rates of crimes of a serious nature, such as murder, assault, robbery, and theft, have likewise shown a systematic upward tendency. In the "normal" course of

---

[25] Ibid., 554–55; Cipolla, *Before the Industrial Revolution,* 39.
[26] Cipolla, *Before the Industrial Revolution,* 54–55; Flora, *State Economy and Society in Western Europe,* chap. 8 and 454.
[27] See Mitchell, *European Historical Statistics 1750–1970,* 16ff.
[28] See A. C. Carlson, *Family Questions* (New Brunswick, N.J.: Transaction Publishers, 1992); idem, *The Swedish Experiment* (New Brunswick, N.J.: Transaction Publishers, 1993); idem, "What Has Government Done to Our Families?" *Essays in Political Economy* 13 (Auburn: Ludwig von Mises Institute, 1991); Ch. Murray, *Losing Ground* (New York: Basic Books, 1984); also J. A. Schumpter, *Capitalism, Socialism, and Democracy* (New York: Harper, 1942), chap. 14.

events, that is, with rising standards of living, it can be expected that the protection against social disasters such as crime will undergo continual improvement, just as one would expect the protection against natural disasters to become progressively better. Indeed, throughout the Western world, this appears to have been the case by and large until recently when, during the second half of the twentieth century, crime rates began to climb steadily upward.[29]

To be sure, there are a number of factors other than increased irresponsibility and shortsightedness brought on by legislation and public welfare that may contribute to crime. Men commit more crimes than women, the young more than the old, blacks more than whites, and city dwellers more than villagers. There is, however, a systematic relationship between high time preference and crime. Consequently, if the social degrees of time preference increases, the frequency of serious crime should rise, as in fact has happened.[30]

From the vantage point of elementary economic theory and in light of historical evidence, then, a second lesson follows: a plea for de–democratization.

Such a plea is not one for a return to the *ancien régime*. The legitimacy of monarchical rule appears to have been irretrievably lost. Nor would such a return be a genuine solution, for monarchies, whatever their relative merits, *do* exploit and do squander the earnings of their subjects. Rather, the idea of democratic republicanism must be rendered laughable by identifying it as the source of steadily increased government exploitation and waste. More importantly, however, the idea of the positive alternative of a natural order must be spelled out and a strategy of how to actualize it must be outlined.[31]

On the one hand, this involves the insight that it is not exploitation, either monarchical or democratic, but private property, production, and voluntary exchange that are the ultimate sources of human civilization. On the other hand, in order to approach the goal of a nonexploitative social order, which we may call private property anarchy, the idea of majoritarianism should be turned against democratic rule itself. Under any form of government, even under democracy, the ruling class makes up only a small proportion of the total population. Given this fact, it would appear possible to persuade a majority of the voters that it is adding insult to injury to let those living from other peoples' taxes have a say in how high these taxes are. The majority of voters could decide, democratically, to take the right to vote away from all government employees and everyone who receives government benefits, whether they are welfare recipients or professors at state–funded universities.

Moreover, in conjunction with this strategy, it is necessary to recognize the overriding importance of secession. Secession always involves the breaking away of a smaller from a larger population. It is thus a vote against the consolidating tendency

---

[29] See J. Q. Wilson and R. J. Herrnstein, *Crime and Human Nature* (New York: Simon & Schuster, 1985), 408–09; on the magnitude of the increase in criminal activity brought about by democratic republicanism and welfarism in the course of the last 100 years, R. D. McGrath, *Gunfighters, Highwaymen, and Vigilantes* (Berkeley: University of California Press, 1984), esp. chap. 13.

[30] On the relationship between high time preference and crime, see E. C. Banfield, *The Unheavenly City Revisited* (Boston: Little, Brown & Company, 1974), esp. chaps. 3 and 8; idem, "Present–Orientedness and Crime," *Assessing the Criminal,* ed. R. E. Barnett and J. Hagel (Cambridge: Ballinger, 1977); Wilson and Herrnstein, *Crime and Human Nature,* 414–24.

[31] See H. H. Hoppe, "The Political Economy of Monarchy and Democracy and the Idea of a Natural Order," *Journal of Libertarian Studies* 11, no. 2 (1995).

of democracy and majoritarianism. Provided that the process of secession results in small enough political units, it becomes possible for a few individuals, based on the popular recognition of their economic independence, outstanding professional achievement, morally impeccable personal life, superior judgment and taste, and courage, to rise to the rank of natural, voluntarily acknowledged authorities who lend legitimacy to the idea of a natural order of competing (nonmonopolistic) judges and overlapping jurisdictions. Such a pattern exists even now in the arena of international trade and travel, which is a pure private–law society, and could be instituted more pervasively as the answer to monarchy *and* democracy.

Lesson Three: Against Relativism (Positivism)

There are no immutable laws of history. The events of the past were neither inevitable, nor is our future written in stone. Rather, history as well the future course of events has been and will be determined by ideas, both true and false. The formation of states, the tendency toward political centralization, the transition from monarchical to democratic rule, as well as the resistance to governmental exploitation, the peaceful or violent overthrow of governments, secessionist movements, and the continued existence of a system of anarchical relations within the sphere of international politics and trade (the absence of a world government) were and are the result of changing and conflicting ideas, and the relative distribution and strength of these ideas in the minds of individuals.

The history of the West, and the outstanding role of the Western world in human history, is intertwined with two uniquely Western intellectual contributions: Greek rationalism and Christianity. The West has come to incorporate Greek and Christian ideas, and then, as a result of Renaissance, Reformation, Counterreformation, Enlightenment, and Romanticism, the successive disintegration and devolution of their synthesis into the present ideology of Secular Relativism (Positivism).

Classical Greek thought, culminating in the work of Aristotle, contributed a thorough rationalist attitude to the West: the view of man as a *rational* animal, the highest respect for logic and logical reasoning, a strong belief in the existence of natural law and the intelligibility of nature and man, and a firm realism and "this–worldliness." However, as the by–product of rationalism, Greece also produced Sophism, Skepticism, and Relativism.[32]

Mainstream Christianity, after confused beginnings and numerous abortive schisms stemming from major inconsistencies and contradictions in the system of the Holy Scriptures, adopted Greek this–worldliness (if only as a temporal, and transitory end); it affirmed the *Genesis* passage "Be fruitful, and multiply, and replenish the earth, and subdue it; and have dominion over the fish of the sea, and over the fowl of the air, and over every living think that moveth upon the earth"; and it adopted the Greeks' high regard for rationality and a firm belief in the intelligibility of nature and man and in the possibility of human progress. Mainstream Christianity made several other unique contributions. Even more than Greek paganism, Christian monotheism placed emphasis on logical consistency and on the idea of the universality of law and the unity of thought. In addition, in viewing each man as created in the divine image, Christianity gave the Greek idea of natural law a decisively individualistic turn. Natural

---

[32] See Rothbard, *Economic Thought Before Adam Smith*, chap. 1.

human rights in particular became *individual* human rights, which applied equally to *every* human being and united all of mankind in a single oecumene.

Moreover, mainstream Christianity gradually freed itself of its largely cultist beginnings when the basic Christian unit was a sect, based on communal or even communist property ownership and controlled by a cult leader or hierarchy of leaders. Influenced by its long contact with Rome and the Roman family and kinship system, mainstream Christianity accepted the individual family and the private household as the basic unit of civil life (and communal ownership was relegated to monasteries and monastic life). Furthermore, the family provided the model of the Christian social order. Just as a hierarchical order existed in each family, so there was a hierarchical order within the Christian community of children, parents, priests, bishops, archbishops, cardinals, the Pope, and finally the transcendent God as the Father in heaven. Likewise, regarding earthly affairs, society was viewed as a quasifamilial hierarchy of free holders, knights, vassals, lords, and feudal kings, tied together by an elaborate system of kinship relations. And analogous to the supremacy of spiritual values in the family, the earthly power of lords and kings was held to be subordinate and subject to the ultimate, spiritual–intellectual authority of priests, bishops, the pope, and ultimately, God.

In effect, this combination of individualism, universalism, the family and kinship orientation, the acknowledgement of a multilayered social rank order and the recognition of the supremacy of the universal—supraterritorial—Church over any particular lord or king shaped Christianity into a powerful ideological weapon against the growth of state power.[33] However, Christian doctrine as embodied in Scholastic philosophy suffered from an inescapable internal contradiction. Scholasticism did not succeed in bridging the gulf between belief and revealed dogma, on the one hand, and knowledge and intelligibility, on the other. Hence, its acceptance of rationalism was ultimately only conditional.[34] As a result of a series of ideological challenges, the Scholastic system slowly disintegrated, and the ideological bulwark that it once provided against the encroachment of state power gradually eroded.

With the Renaissance, Greek paganism and secularism returned to the ideological scene. Moral relativism spread, and ideologues of unlimited state power such as Machiavelli rose to prominence, preparing the intellectual ground for numerous local tyrants and despots. Attention shifted away from the sciences. Mysticism flourished. Increased emphasis was placed on the arts, and, as a reflection of the newly found "freedom from" religious and moral constraints, the arts became increasingly profane and sensual, as in the erotic paintings of Correggio and the writings of Boccaccio and Rabelais.[35]

In ideological reaction to these "decadent" tendencies, which had also affected the mainstream Church, the Reformation brought a sharp return to religion. However,

---

[33] See Lord Action, *Essays in the History of Liberty* (Indianapolis: Liberty Fund, 1985), chap. 2; Rothbard, *Economic Thought Before Adam Smith,* chaps. 2–4; R. Nisbet, *Prejudices* (Cambridge: Harvard University Press, 1982), 110ff.

[34] See L. v. Mises, *Theory and History* (Auburn, Ala.: Ludwig von Mises Institute, 1985), 44ff.; E. Cassirer, *The Myth of the State* (New Haven: Yale University Press), chap. VII.

[35] See A. Ruestow, *Freedom and Domination. A Historical Critique of Civilization* (Princeton, N.J.: Princeton University Press, 1980), 256–67; Nisbet, *Prejudices,* 261ff.; Rothbard, *Economic Thought Before Adam Smith,* chap. 6; Q. Skinner, *The Foundations of Modern Political Thought* 1 (Cambridge: Cambridge University Press, 1978).

the new Protestant religiosity was decidedly reactionary: antirationalist and egalitarian. Faith, held to be the sole path to salvation, was viewed as the foundation of Christianity, whereas that "harlot reason," as Luther called it, was held in contempt. God's will was considered unintelligible and irrational; the Augustinian doctrine of human predestination was revived; the fate of each person was held to be dependent upon the grace of God and His unfathomable decree. At the same time, the Bible was elevated to the rank of the highest religious authority, and the idea of a "universal priesthood," based on everyone's personal Bible reading and unmediated through the spiritual hierarchy of the Church, was promoted. Each person came to be viewed as an independent and equal religious authority, subject only to his own conscience. The formerly established distinction between a secular life and an institutionally separate religious life of priests and monks was erased, and all of life was viewed as an exercise in Christian faith.[36]

As a result of antirationalism, the development of the sciences suffered, and literature and the arts declined. Even more momentous, however, were the effects of Protestant egalitarianism. Not only did it lead to the destruction of the unity of the Church, but without any recognizable spiritual ranks, that is, with the democratization of religious authority, the Protestant movement quickly disintegrated into numerous branches. Long submerged strands of early Christianity, such as Millenarianism, Anabaptism, and Communism, resurfaced. The proliferation of religious confessions, cults, and sects, incompatible with each another but each grounded in the Holy Scripture as the highest authority and hermetically shielded from all rational inquiry, promoted social disintegration, mutual hostility, and finally warfare on a scale and of a brutality unsurpassed in the West until the late nineteenth and the twentieth centuries.[37] Moreover, in breaking up the unity of the Catholic Church and undermining the idea of a spiritual rank order, the Protestant revolution isolated and weakened the individual vis-à-vis earthly rulers. The rulers, relieved of the countervailing authority of a universal Church and its hierarchy, eagerly exploited this opportunity for an expansion of state power by establishing numerous territorial Churches and by merging the secular and the ecclesiastic powers in their own hands.

The Counterreformation duplicated within the remaining Catholic world what the Reformation had accomplished for the Protestant world. Everywhere, formerly weak feudal kings became mighty, absolute monarchs.[38] In reaction to Reformation and Counterreformation, then, the seventeenth- and eighteenth-century Enlightenment brought a decisive return of rationalism. But the rationalism of the Enlightenment suffered—and ultimately succumbed—because of two fundamental flaws. On the one hand, in reaction to the religious fervor stirred by the Reformation and the Counterreformation, the rationalism of the Enlightenment was significantly *anti*-clerical and even *anti*-Christian. On the other hand, influenced by the Protestantism, it was a decisively *egalitarian* rationalism.[39]

The recognition of the supremacy and autonomy of reason and a renewed interest in both Stoic philosophy and late Scholasticism (Molina, Suarez, Mariana) led to the development of a new secular, purely rational natural rights doctrine centered on the notions of self-ownership, private property, and contract: to Althusius, Grotius,

---

[36] See Ruestow, *Freedom and Domination*, 267–87.
[37] See J. F. C. Fuller, *The Conduct of War* (New York: Da Capo, 1992), chap. 1.
[38] See Rothbard, *Economic Though Before Adam Smith*, chap. 5.
[39] See Ruestow, *Freedom and Domination*, 301–26; Cassirer, *The Myth of the State*, chap. XIV.

Pufendorf, Locke, Thomasius, and Wolff. The earthly ruler was seen as subject to the same universal and eternal principles of justice as everyone else, and a state either would derive its justification from a "contract" between private property owners or it could not be justified.[40] There remained significant differences as regards the precise meaning of "contract" (Did it bind only the original signers? Could it be revoked?), but there can be little doubt that, under the growing ideological influence of the natural rights doctrine, the power of kings became increasingly constrained.[41]

However, owing to its anti–clericalism (as in Voltaire, for instance) and its egalitarianism, which went as far as to deny all innate differences among human beings and believed all men to be equally capable of rational thought (as in Helvetius and, under empiricist auspices, Locke, for instance), Enlightenment rationalism committed a fatal sociological error. It was blind to the fact that, in the real world, where men are *not* equal, its ideal of a purely contractual society based on the institution of private property could be maintained and defended against internal or external assault and invasion only if a society possessed a distinctly hierarchical structure, that is, a voluntarily acknowledged rank order of horizontally and vertically interconnected intermediary institutions and authorities; and that Christianity and the hierarchy of the Church would have to function as one of the more important of these intermediary authorities.[42] Misled by its anticlericalism and egalitarianism, Enlightenment rationalism furthered the tendency, begun with the Protestant Revolution, of isolating the individual vis–à–vis worldly rulers: of eliminating all intermediate authorities and subjecting each individual equally and directly to the sole authority of the state, thereby promoting the centralization of state power.

The fundamental sociological error of this view was revealed by the events of the French Revolution. When the absolute monarchy finally collapsed to the applause of almost all Enlightenment philosophers, nothing was left to fill the existing power vacuum. The authority and economic independence of the Church was ruined, and all formerly existing feudal bonds and institutions were destroyed. Consequently, to the consternation of most of the Enlightenment, the Revolution quickly degenerated into chaos, mob rule, terror, dictatorship, nationalist aggression, and, finally, the restoration of the *ancien régime*.

As a result, the Enlightenment's rationalist philosophy was thoroughly discredited. In reaction to the French Revolution and the Enlightenment, and inspired by prerevolutionary writers such as Jean-Jacques Rousseau, Romanticism came to hold sway.[43] Natural law theory was thrown out. According to the Romantic world view, no absolutely and universally true human rights and social laws existed. History, rather than theory, became the center of attention. Each individual, each tribe, and each people was viewed as having its own unique history; and because no absolute standards of right and wrong existed, each history was held to be of equal worth (historical relativism). History was studied neither to pass judgment on the past nor to learn anything for the future, but solely to reveal the diversity of mankind and

---

[40] See Cassirer, *The Myth of the State*, chap. XIII; Ruestow, *Freedom and Domination*, 301–26.

[41] See also J. Tuck, *Natural Rights Theories* (Cambridge: Cambridge University Press, 1979); Rothbard, *Economic Thought Before Adam Smith*, esp. 369ff.

[42] See W. Roepke, *Die Gesellschaftskrisis der Gegenwart* (Erlenbach: E. Rentsch, 4942), chap. 4, esp. 74 ff.; also Mises, *Theory and History*, 47f.

[43] See Ruestow, *Freedom and Domination*, 343–6ff; Cassirer, *The Myth of the State*, chap. XIV; Mises, *Theory and History*, chap. 40.

human tradition (multiculturalism). Devoid of any theory, history possessed no practical purpose or implication. It was studied for its own sake, with the sole purpose of "inner" intellectual enrichment. Likewise, each religion was seen to possess a right of its own: mysticism, Platonism, Buddhism, paganism, and deism no less than Christianity; and religiosity, too, was viewed as an entirely private affair, as a matter of "inner" choice without any practical implications. Instead of viewing knowledge and beliefs as tools of action, Romanticism considered them instruments of aesthetic or poetic expression, and the Romantic attitude toward the external world of physical events was one of passive contemplation, quietism, withdrawal, resignation, or even fatalism. The outside world was held to be unintelligible, driven by irrational or mystic forces, and ultimately of no concern. The only matter of genuine importance was each person's "inner" freedom of thought and imagination.

Not surprisingly, the power of the state grew with the influence of Romanticism.[44] If history is viewed as the source and origin of "right," then any state is undoubtedly "just"; and if state power increases, it cannot do so except by "historical right." Accordingly, the state and the growth of state power should always be met with a contemplative attitude of resigned acceptance. What better message could a ruler want to hear? Due to a gaping hole within the Romantic world view, however, its influence soon faded into the background, to be complemented and finally overshadowed by Positivism, the dominant philosophical paradigm of our age.

The romantic outlook suffered from the obvious defect that, even if one accepted it as plausible for the social world, it still could not account for the existence of the natural sciences and technology. Clearly, these did not derive their justification from history, and the study of nature and technology (unlike that of society) was not disinterested and undertaken for its own sake. Rather, the natural sciences and technology apparently derived their justification from their *present practical success*. Within this realm at least, identifiable progress existed, and it was definitely *not* the case that each historical era or episode could be regarded as equally right and worthy. Positivism offered an attractive way out of these ideological difficulties.

Influenced by eighteenth–century empiricism, in particular by Hume, nineteenth– and twentieth–century Positivism shared most of its antirationalist assumptions with the Romantics. Like the Romantics, but in sharp contrast to rationalist Enlightenment, the Positivists rejected the idea of a rational ethic and a natural rights theory. Value judgments were viewed as arbitrary, a matter of personal taste, and incapable of rational justification. Reason was not the master, but the slave of the passions. Natural rights theory in particular was nothing but nonsensical metaphysics. Indeed, insofar as any difference existed between Romanticism and Positivism, it consisted of the fact that the moral relativism of the Positivists was apparently even more extreme and far–reaching. Whereas the Romantics relativized religion, they still recognized the value of *some* religion; and, while the Romantics denied the existence of absolute values, they still valued history and tradition. In contrast, the Positivisim, in this respect very much like Enlightenment rationalism, was decidedly secularist (religion was held to be merely hocus–pocus) and unhistorical (the past possessed no special value).

Positivism shared with Romanticism the relativistic view that reason is incapable of recognizing any necessarily universal and immutable positive (causal) laws. Indeed, the denial of the very possibility of, in Kantian terminology, true synthetic *a*

---

[44] See L. v. Mises, *Socialism* (Indianapolis: Liberty Fund, 1981), esp. 419ff.; M. N. Rothbard, *Freedom, Inequality, Primitivism, and the Division of Labor* (Auburn: Ludwig von Mises Institute, 1991).

priori propositions is one of the cornerstones of Positivism.[45] According to Positivism, no such thing as nonhypothetically true positive (empirical) laws exists. In other words, nothing about reality can be known to be true *a priori*. Rather, all empirical knowledge is hypothetical knowledge, and all nonhypothetical knowledge is analytical knowledge which contains no empirical information whatsoever but consists merely of arbitrary symbolic conventions and definitions. The only difference between the Positivist and the Romantic relativisms was a psychological one. The Romantic's relativism was that of an artists, that is, a poet, novelist, or historian, whose subject matter was the inner world of meaning, purpose, expression, and emotion. Accordingly, he tended to view individuals as *different* (unique), and he approached his subject matter in a *passive* mode to develop his private appreciation, empathy, or sympathy. In contrast, the Positivist's relativism was that of an engineer, an experimental physicist, or a chemist. His subject matter was the external physical world of sensory data, and he tended to view individuals as *identical* (equal). He approached his subject matter with an *activist* attitude, one of physical manipulation and interference.

In fact, as can be seen from the Positivists' conception of logic, it cannot be claimed that Positivist relativism is even *less* relativistic. While the Romantics viewed logic and deductive reasoning as on a par with intuition and mythical revelation, the Positivists considered it as empty of all empirical content. However, due to its activistic (experimental) attitude, Positivistic philosophy at least appeared to make room for the idea of *a posteriori* law—of trial and error, hypothetical conjecture, confirmation and refutation—and, hence, of the possibility of scientific progress (as manifested in the field of the natural sciences).[46]

If the contemplative relativism of the Romantics had been good for the health of the state and the growth of state power, the growing influence of the activist relativism of the Positivists proved to be even better. According to Positivism, ethics is not a cognitive discipline. No normative statement has any better foundation than any other such statement. But then, what is wrong with everyone trying to enforce and impose on others whatever one wishes? Surely nothing; everything goes. Ethics is reduced to the problem of what one "can get away with" doing. What better message could there be for those in power? It is precisely what they want to hear: might is and makes right!

Similarly, they will be thrilled about the message of Positivism as regards the social sciences. In the realm of the natural sciences, the Positivist doctrine is relatively harmless. It has not, nor could it have, fundamentally changed the course of the natural sciences. However, the same cannot be said about the social sciences. Under the growing influence of Positivism, economics in particular has been destroyed beyond recognition, and this once powerful ideological fortress against the encroachment of state power has been removed.[47]

---

[45] See L. Kolakowski, *Die Philosophie des Positivismus* (Muenchen: Piper, 1971); H. H. Hoppe, *Kritik der kausalwissenschaftlichen Sozialforschung* (Opladen: Westdeutscher Verlag, 1983); idem, *The Economics and Ethics of Private Property*, pt. II; Mises, *Theory and History*, chap. 11; idem, *The Ultimate Foundation of Economic Science* (Kansas City, Kans.: Sheed, Andrews & McMeel, 1978); B. Blanshard, *Reason and Analysis* (LaSalle: Open Court, 1964).

[46] Strictly speaking, even this impression is fallacious. For how can it be possible to see two or more observational experiences as *falsifying* or *confirming* each other rather than as mere isolated experiences?

[47] See H. H. Hoppe, "Austrian Rationalism in the Age of the Decline of Positivism," *Journal des Economistes et des Etudes Humaines* 2, no. 2/3 (1991).

From the Christian Middle Ages through Spanish Scholasticism to the seventeenth and eighteenth centuries of Enlightenment, parallel to and intertwined with the development of "normative" natural rights theory, a systematic body of economic theory developed, culminating in the writings of Cantillon and Turgot. According to this intellectual tradition—carried on in the nineteenth century by Say, Senior, Cairnes, Menger, and Boehm–Bawerk, and in the twentieth century by Mises, Robbins, and Rothbard—economics was viewed as a "logic of action." Starting with self–evident propositions and combining these with a few empirical and empirically testable assumptions, economics was conceived as an axiomatic–deductive science and economic theorems as propositions which were at the same time realistic and nonhypothetically or *a priori* true.[48] Consider, for instance, the following economic propositions: In every voluntary exchange, both partners must expect to profit, they must evaluate the things to be exchanged as having unequal value, and they must have opposite preference orders. Or: Whenever an exchange is not voluntary, but coerced, such as highway robbery or taxation, one exchange party benefits at the expense of the other. Or: Whenever minimum wage laws are enforced that require wage rates to be higher than existing market wages, involuntary unemployment will result. Or: Whenever the quantity of money is increased while the demand for money remains unchanged, the purchasing power of money will fall. Or: Any supply of money is equally, "optimal," such that no increase in the money supply can raise the overall standard of living (while it can have redistributive effects). Or: Collective ownership of all factors of production makes cost accounting impossible, and hence leads to permanent misallocations. Or: Taxation of income producers, other things remaining the same, raises their effective rate of time preference, and hence leads to a lower output of goods produced. Apparently, these theorems contain knowledge about reality, and yet they do not seem to be hypothetical (empirically falsifiable) proposition but rather true by definition.

According to Positivism, however, this cannot be so. Insofar as these propositions claim to be empirically meaningful, they must be hypotheses, forever subject to empirical confirmation or falsification. One could formulate the very opposite of the above propositions without thereby stating anything can be recognized from the outset, *a priori*, as false and nonsensical. Experience will have to decide the matter. Thus, in assuming the Positivist doctrine, the highway robber, taxman, union official, or chairman of the Federal Reserve Board would act legitimately, from a scientific point of view, in claiming that taxation benefits the taxed and increases productive output, minimum wage laws increase employment, and the creation of paper money generates all–around prosperity. As a good Positivist, one would have to admit that these are merely hypotheses. With the predicted effects being "beneficial," however, they surely should be tested. After all, one would not close one's eyes to new experience, and one would always be willing to react flexibly and open mindedly, contingent upon the outcome of such experience. Yet, if the outcome is not as hypothesized, and the robbed or taxed do not appear to benefit, employment actually decreases, or economic cycles rather than all–around prosperity ensue, one can always take recourse, "scientifically legitimate," to the possibility of "immunizing" one's hypoth-

---

[48] See M. N. Rothbard, *Individualism and the Philosophy of the Social Sciences* (San Francisco, Calif.: Cato Institute, 1979); H. H. Hoppe, *Praxeology and Economic Science* (Auburn: Ludwig von Mises Institute, 1988).

eses. For whatever empirical evidence one brings forward against them, as soon as one adopts Positivism, the robber's or the taxman's case is safe from decisive criticism, because any failure can always be ascribed to some as yet uncontrolled intervening variable. Not even the most perfectly conducted experiment could change this situation because it would never be possible to control all variables that might conceivably have some influence on the variable to be explained or the result to be produced. No matter what the charges brought against the robber, the taxman, or the chairman of the Federal Reserve Board, Positivist philosophy will always allow each to preserve and rescue the "hard core" of his "research program." Experience merely informs us that a particular experiment did not reach its goal, but it can never tell us if a slightly different experiment will produce any different results. Why, then, would the robber, the taxman, or the chairman of the Federal Reserve Board *not* want to play down all apparently falsifying experiences as merely accidental, so long as they can personally profit from conducting their robbing, taxing, or money–creating experiments? Why would he *not* want to interpret all apparent falsifications as experiences that were produced by some unfortunately neglected circumstance and that would disappear or turn into their very opposite, revealing the "true" relationship between taxes, minimum wage laws, the creation of money, and prosperity, once these circumstances were controlled?[49]

The attitude toward economics that Positivism fuels is that of a relativist social engineer whose motto is "nothing can be known with certainty to be impossible within the realm of social phenomena and there is nothing that one might not want to try out on one's fellowmen, so long as one keeps an open mind." Not surprisingly, this message was quickly recognized by the powers that be as a mighty ideological weapon in the pursuit of their goal of increasing their control over civil society and of enriching themselves at the expense of others. Accordingly, lavish support was bestowed on the Positivist movement, and this movement returned the favor by destroying ethics and economics as the traditional bastions of social rationalism. It eradicated from public consciousness a vast body of knowledge that had once constituted a seemingly permanent part of the heritage of Western thought and civilization, paving the ideological ground of the twentieth century as the "age of unlimited social experimentation."[50]

In light of the history of Western philosophy, then, a third lesson follows: a plea for a return to rationalism. Such a plea is neither a plea for a return to the Aristotelian–Christian rationalism of Thomistic and Scholastic philosophy, nor a plea for a return to the peculiar rationalism of the Enlightenment. As the legitimacy of monarchical rule has waned, the same may be true for Christianity and the Christian Church. In Nietzsche's words, "Gott ist tot." Nor would a return to the Christian past be desirable, for Christian rationalism was never more than conditional. Instead, it might be possible to embrace the rationalism expounded more than three centuries ago by Grotius. "Even the will of an omnipotent being," wrote Grotius, "cannot change the

---

[49] See H. H. Hoppe, *A Theory of Socialism and Capitalism* (Boston: Kluwer, 1989), chap. 6.

[50] See Mises, *Human Action*, pt. 7; idem, *The Ultimate Foundation of Economic Science,* esp. chaps. 5–8, which conclude with the verdict: "As far as the empiricist principle of logical positivism refers to the experimental methods of the natural sciences, it merely asserts what is not questioned by anybody. As far as it rejects the epistemological principles of the sciences of human action, it is not only entirely wrong. It is also knowingly and intentionally undermining the intellectual foundations of Western civilization" (133).

principles of morality or abrogate those fundamental rights that are guaranteed by natural laws. These laws would maintain their objective validity even if we should assume—*per impossible*—that there is no God or that he does not care for human affairs."[51]

In contrast to Enlightenment rationalism, the rationalism to be restored will have to be unconditional *and* decidedly *non*–egalitarian. It must be a rationalism that recognizes, as a primordial fact, the existence of fundamental inequalities between human beings. This fact should be celebrated as the foundation of the division of labor and of human civilization. Furthermore, as a result of the diversity of human talents, in every society of any degree of complexity, a few individuals, owing to their superior achievements in terms of wealth, wisdom, bravery, or a combination thereof, will acquire the status of a "natural elite"; and, because of selective mating and marriage and the laws of civil and genetic inheritance, the status as a member of the natural elite will more likely than not be passed on within a relatively few families. It must also be openly acknowledged that the existence of social hierarchies and ranks of authority is not only logically compatible with the idea of the universality of ethical and economic law, but constitutes the sociological presupposition of their very recognition.[52]

To maintain that no such thing as a rational ethic exists does not imply "tolerance" and "pluralism," as champions of positivism such as Milton Friedman falsely claim, and moral absolutism does not imply "intolerance" and "dictatorship."[53] To the contrary, without absolute values "tolerance" and "pluralism" are just other arbitrary ideologies, and there is no reason to accept them rather than any others such as cannibalism and slavery. Only if absolute values, such as a human right of self–ownership, exist, that is, only if "pluralism" or "tolerance" are not merely among a multitude of tolerable values, can pluralism and tolerance in fact be safeguarded.[54]

Nor is it true, as Friedman suggests, that the Positivist view regarding all empirical knowledge as merely hypothetical implies intellectual "modesty," whereas those holding the opposite view are guilty of intellectual "hubris." It is the other way around. If all nonhypothetical knowledge is empirically meaningless and if analytic knowledge and all empirical knowledge is hypothetical knowledge, then what about the

---

[51] See Cassirer, *The Myth of the State,* 172; Rothbard, *Economic Thought Before Adam Smith,* 72.
[52] See W. Roepke, *Jenseits von Angebot und Nachfrage* (Bern: P. Haupt, 1979), 191–99; idem, *Die Gesellschaftskrise der Gegenwart,* 52f.; Jouvenel, *On Power,* chap. 17; Hoppe, "The Political Economy of Monarchy and Democracy and the Idea of Natural Order."
[53] On Friedman's pronouncements, see M. Friedman, "Say No to Intolerance," *Liberty* 4, no. 6 (July 1991); also J. D. Hammond, "An Interview with Milton Friedman on Methodology," *Research in the History of Economic Thought and Methodology* 10 (Greenwood: JAI Press, 1992), esp 100–02; for another prominent proponent of the same view, see T. W. Hutchison, *The Politics and Philosophy of Economics* (New York: New York University Press, 1981), esp. 196–97.
[54] It is Milton Friedman, and not the targets of his attacks, the "extremist" and "intolerant" Ludwig von Mises and Murray N. Rothbard, who finds himself in the company of dictators. Thus wrote Benito Mussolini in 1921: "If relativism signifies contempt for fixed categories and men who claim to be the bearers of an objective, immortal truth...then there is nothing more relativistic than Fascist attitudes and activity.... From the fact that all ideologies are of equal value, that all ideologies are mere fictions, the modern relativist infers that everybody has the right to create for himself his own ideology and to attempt to enforce it with all the energy of which he is capable." Quoted in H. B. Veatch, *Rational Man. A Modern Interpretation of Aristotelian Ethics* (Bloomington: Indiana University Press, 1962), 41.

status of *this* proposition? If it is taken to be analytic, it is nothing but an arbitrary definition without any empirical content. Any other definition would be equally good (and empty). If it is assumed to be empirically meaningful, it is a hypothesis according to which empirical knowledge is hypothetical knowledge and empirical tests are tests of hypothetical knowledge. Any other hypothesis or any other empirical test or inference is then equally possible. Finally, if the proposition is taken to be empirically meaningful and yet apodictically, categorically, nonhypothetically, or *a priori* true, the Positivist doctrine turns out to be self-contradictory nonsense. This is hardly modesty, but outright intellectual permissiveness!

In contrast, if the existence of nonhypothetical empirical knowledge is admitted, this does not imply that *all* or even most empirical knowledge is of this kind but only that one can distinguish between both types of empirical knowledge, and that this distinction and the delineation of two kinds of empirical questions and answers is itself a nonhypothetically true empirical distinction. Moreover, contrary to the Positivistic permissiveness of "nothing is certain" and "everything is possible" and its disregard or even contempt for the study of history, to assume the existence of nonhypothetical empirical knowledge implies basic intellectual modesty. For if nonhypothetical laws exist, such laws should be expected to be "old" truths discovered long ago. "Newly" discovered nonhypothetical laws, while obviously not impossible, should be rare intellectual events, and the "newer" they appear, the more "suspect" should they be. Hence, the rationalist attitude is one of intellectual humility and respect for the history of thought (and of philosophy and economics in particular).[55] Most nonhypothetical empirical knowledge can be expected to already exist and, at worst, stands in need of being rediscovered (rather than newly invented). That is, in the realm of the nonhypothetical empirical sciences such as philosophy, logic, mathematics, ethics, and economics, scientific "progress" must be expected to be extremely slow and painstaking, and the "danger" is not so much that nothing new and better is added to the existing body of knowledge, as that an already existing body of knowledge is only incompletely relearned or forgotten.

In accordance with this fundamental intellectual humility, the rationalist answer to the Positivistic destruction of ethics (as nonscientific) and economics (as either empirically empty or else hypothetical), while apparently largely forgotten or unlearned, is anything but "new," and while it has surprisingly radical implications, these can hardly be characterized as "dictatorial" or "extremist."[56]

Every person owns his own body as well as all nature-given goods which he puts to use with the help of his body before anyone else does. This ownership implies the right to employ these resources however one sees fit so long as one does not thereby uninvitedly change the physical integrity of another's property or delimit another's physical control over it without his consent. In particular, once a good has first been appropriated or homesteaded by mixing one's labor with it (this being Locke's phrase), then ownership of it can only be acquired by means of a voluntary (contractual) transfer of its property title from a previous to a later owner. These rights of a person

---

[55] On the intellectual modesty of rationalism, see E. Cassirer, *The Myth of the State,* chap. XIII.

[56] Illustrative of the works of the two outstanding social rationalists of the twentieth century, see Mises, *Human Action* and *Theory and History*; and M. N. Rothbard, *Man, Economy, and State* (Los Angeles: Nash, 1972); *The Ethics of Liberty; Economic Thought Before Adam Smith;* and *Classical Economics.*

are absolute. Any person's infringement on them is subject to lawful prosecution by the victim of this infringement or his agent, and it is actionable in accordance with the principles of strict liability and the proportionality of punishment.

These ancient principles are not only intuitively just. Even children and primitives seem to have no trouble recognizing their truth. In fact, is it not plainly absurd to claim that a person should *not* be the owner of his body and those nature–given goods that he had appropriated and produced before anyone else came along? Who else, if not he, should be their owner? Moreover, these principles can be "proven" to be indisputably, that is, nonhypothetically, true and valid. For if a person A were not the owner of his body and all goods originally appropriated, produced, or voluntarily acquired by him, there would only exist two alternatives. Either *anther* person, B, must then be regarded as the owner of A and the goods appropriated, produced, or contractually acquired by A, or both parties, B *and* B, must be regarded as equal co–owners of both bodies and goods. In the first case, A would be B's slave and an object of exploitation. B owns A and the goods originally appropriated, produced, or acquired by A, but A does not own B and the goods homesteaded, produced, or acquired by B. With this rule, two distinct classes of people are created, viz., exploiters (B) and exploited (A), to whom different "law" applies. Hence, this rule fails the "universalization test" and is from the outset disqualified as even a potential human ethic. In order to be able to claim a rule to be a "law," it is necessary that such a rule be universally valid for everyone.

In the second case of universal co–ownership, the requirement of equal rights for everyone is obviously fulfilled. However, this alternative suffers from another, literally fatal flaw, for each activity of a person requires the employment of scarce goods (at least the person's body and its standing room). Yet if all goods were collective property, then no one, at no time and no place, could ever do anything with anything unless he had every other co–owner's prior permission to do what he wanted to do. And how can one give such a permission if one is not even the sole owner of one's own body (and vocal chords)? If one were to follow this rule, mankind would die out instantly. Whatever this is, it is certainly not a *human* ethic. Thus, one is left with the initial principles of self–ownership and first use first ownership (original appropriation, homesteading). They pass the universalization tests, that is, they hold for everyone equally, *and* they can at the same time assure the survival of mankind. They and *only* they are therefore nonhypothetically true ethical rules.

Likewise, the rationalist answer to Positivist economics is old and clear. As long as persons act in accordance with the principles of self–ownership and original appropriation, "social welfare" will invariably be "optimized." A self–owning person's original appropriation of unowned resources increases his welfare (at least *ex ante*), otherwise it would not have been carried out. At the same time, it makes no one worse off, because in appropriating them he takes nothing away from others. Obviously, others could have homesteaded these resources, too, if only they had perceived them as scarce and valuable. Yet, they did not do so, which demonstrates that they attached no value to them whatsoever. Thus, they also cannot be said to have suffered a welfare loss on account of this act. Proceeding from this basis, any further act of production utilizing one's body and homesteaded resources establishes ownership rights to the products created thereby, provided that it does not uninvitedly impair the physical integrity of the body and the resources homesteaded or produced with homesteaded goods by others. The producer gains utility and no one else loses utility. And finally, every voluntary exchange starting from this basis will take place only if both parties expect to benefit from it. The provision that only the *first* user of a good acquires ownership assures that productive efforts will be as high as possible *at all times*. And the provision that only the *physical* integrity of property is protected (and that a person is liable only for *physical* damage or restrictions upon others' property) guarantees that every owner has a constant incentive to increase the value of his physical property (and to avoid value losses) by means of physically controlled and calculated actions.

Any deviation from these principles implies a redistribution of property titles away from user producers and contractors of goods onto non–users producers and noncontractors. The latter, the exploiters, increase their supply of goods, and thus enhance their welfare, at the expense of a corresponding loss of the wealth and welfare of the exploited. Hence, a lower state of "social welfare" will result. Among the exploited, there will be relatively less original appropriation of resources whose scarcity is recognized, less production of new goods, less maintenance of existing goods, and less mutually beneficial trading and contracting. And among the exploiters, this rule creates a permanent incentive for shortsightedness and wastefulness. For if one group of people is permitted to supplement its future income by means of the expropriation of goods appropriated, produced, or voluntarily acquired by others, its preference for current consumption over saving (future consumption) will be systematically strengthened, and the likelihood of misallocations, miscalculations, and economic losses will be permanently heightened.

Once these old, rationalist principles of ethics and economics are rediscovered under the Positivist rubble, and it is understood again that they are *absolutely*—nonhypothetically, apodictically, categorically, *a priori*—true, the tendencies toward centralization, democratization, and the growth of state power can be critically challenged. For in light of these principles, central governments all around the globe can be recognized for what they are: threats to justice and economic efficiency everywhere. Without justice, these institutions are, as St. Augustine noted, nothing but bands of robbers. If, and *only* if, this recognition of states (governments) as fundamentally unjust and wasteful prevails in the court of public opinion, will the power of the central state devolve on to smaller and smaller territories, and make room for a system of ordered liberty.

Epistemological Circularity as a Justification for Liberal Democracy

Aryeh Botwinick

The Greeks invented both democracy and constitutionalism. Democracy signifies self-rule by the people of a specific polity; constitutionalism denotes a set of norms, of regularized procedures, to limit the scope and impact of democracy. The fusion of democracy with constitutionalism yields what we call "liberal democracy," a concept wherein the notion of "democracy" refers to rule by the people and the adjective "liberal" evokes the panoply of constitutional protections of minority rights. For Sheldon Wolin, democracy and constitutionalism are locked in permanent, irreconcilable tension. Wolin says, "We might think of democracy as resistant to the rationalizing conceptions of power and its organization which for centuries have dominated western thinking and have developed constitutionalism and their legitimating rationale." Continuing in this vein, Wolin examines Greek sources for traces of what he terms "an aconstitutional conception of democracy."[1]

While I sympathize with Wolin's assigning of priority to "democracy" over "constitutionalism," I believe that both can be accommodated by a liberal democratic paradigm that preserves their ties to a particular epistemological and metaphysical framework. There is a persistent anomaly that haunts classical presentations of liberal democratic theory from Hobbes's *Leviathan* to John Rawls's *A Theory of Justice*. The relevant arguments are mostly circular, which is a source of embarrassment to the theorist. Turning to the precursor of these arguments in Plato's *Theaetetus* helps us to see that circularity, far from being a liability, is integral to the case for liberal democracy. Plato's epistemological discussion shows that, whether we start with an immediate sense perception or invoke mind-ordained categories as the primary factors in generating and validating knowledge, we cannot avoid "involving reasoning that uses in the argument or proof a conclusion to be proved or one of its unproved consequences." This recourse to "process" in the *Theaetetus* corresponds to Socrates' self-description as a midwife who helps his interlocutors refine their capacities for reasoning and their formulations without reaching the truth. The mode

---

[1] Sheldon Wolin, "Norm and Form: The Constitutionalization of Democracy," in *Athenian Political Thought and Reconstruction of American Democracy,* J. Peter Euben, John R. Wallach, and Josiad Ober, eds. (Ithaca, N.Y.: Cornell University Press, 1994), 37.

of life sketched and enacted by Socrates implies that we inhabit an ever-expanding middle that repeatedly propels us back to the formulation of beginnings. The skepticism that undergirds the perpetual initiation of inquiry serves as a bridge linking democracy with liberalism. Because our arguments do not transcend circularity, democrats contend, no particular individuals or groups can either claim superior knowledge or persuasively argue against the inclusion of as many people as possible in the making of public decisions. At the same time, because no decision can claim an unreserved epistemological sanction, liberalism introduces a series of braking mechanisms that allow democratic outcomes to be reconsidered and revised. Liberalism, *qua* preoccupation with process in all of the manifold constitutional and institutional senses with which we are familiar in American democracy, facilitates a continuing replenishment and adjustment of democratic content. The emphasis on "process" as a metaphysical concept in the *Theaetetus* gets translated in the historical course of democratic theory into the more narrowly political set of liberal democratic notions according to which no public verdict on any issue can be conceived as final. Majority rule is counterbalanced by minority rights; the content of "rights," in turn, is subject to majority interpretation and redefinition. Under the more expansive, metaphysical reenvisioning of the nature of democracy that I am proposing, it is not only "the people," but also "sovereignty," "truth," and "the ultimate telos of human personal collective life" that serve as what Claude Lefort has called "absent presences" in democratic political life.[2]

"Democratic constitutionalism," says Wolin, "is representative of a moment rather than a teleological form."[3] We might classify democracy that "is representative of a moment" as participatory democracy. In a subsidiary portion of the *Theaetetus* where Plato dwells on some of the ramifications of the protagorean and Heraclitean nexus of ideas, we find a remarkable prefiguration of the metaphysics of participatory democracy. The *Theaetetus* thus provides us with enduring classical models cast in a metaphysical mold of the dominant types of democracy with which we are familiar in our own world, viz., liberal and participatory democracy. In what follows, I shall try to show how arguments concerning circularity generate the liberal democratic model of democracy in the *Theaetetus*. Next, I hope to demonstrate the pervasiveness of circularity in the Platonic dialogues. Finally, I shall plot the derivation of participatory democracy from Plato's *Theaetetus*.

I

In the *Theaetetus,* Plato sets up an ideal typology between two diametrically opposed starting points for Greek philosophy and shows how both terminate in incoherence. Heraclitus and Protagoras had assigned centrality to constant flux and motion and, therefore, also to immediate perception as the source of knowledge. Parmenides had shifted the emphasis to theoretical frameworks (with their extreme heightening in the notion of the One) as enjoying privacy in the generation of knowledge. Plato shows from numerous perspectives how we cannot move from either starting point to the familiar epistemological judgments that we make without presupposing what we are trying to prove.

---

[2] Claude Lefort, *Democracy and Political Theory,* trans. David Macey (Minneapolis: University of Minnesota Press, 1988), 17–19.
[3] Wolin, "Norm and Form," 39–40.

Socrates establishes a conceptual linkage between Protagorean notion that man is the measure of all things and the Heraclitean conception that everything is in flux. Transferred to the field of perception, the idea that man is the measure of all things signifies that "perception is knowledge." "Whatever the individual judges by means of perception is true for him." "No man can assess another's experience better than he, or claim authority to examine another man's judgment and see if it be right or wrong." "Only the individual himself can judge of his own world, and what he judges is always true and correct."[4] What lies behind this Protagorean position is Heraclitean metaphysics. If everything is constantly changing, then what we perceive at any given moment is our only source of knowledge as to what the world is like. Socrates invokes against the Protagorean-Heraclitean position the issue of reflexivity:

> How could it ever be, my friend, that Protagoras was a wise man, so wise as to think himself fit to be the teacher of other men and worth large fees; while we in comparison with him the ignorant ones, needed to go and sit at his feet—we who are ourselves each the measure of his own wisdom. Can we avoid the conclusion that Protagoras was just playing to the crowd when he said this?[5]

Both Protagoras's and Heraclitus's formulations fail to pass tests of reflexivity. Obviously, Protagoras wants his relativist position to hold up against all competitors. But, if "man is the measure of all things," then a philosopher's objectivist, antirelativist position is as much such a measure as Protagoras' own relativist position. On what theoretical, cognitive basis can Protagoras privilege himself in relation to the positions he rejects? Analogously, Heraclitus considers everything to be in flux except his own view that "everything is in flux." How can he close the gap between what his statement officially communicates and his point in making the statement in the first place? Why is his formulation exempt from his own strictures concerning the pervasiveness of flux?

Another casualty of the Protagorean-Heraclitean position is the possibility of genuine disagreement and mutual correction and criticism. "To examine and try to refute each other's appearances and judgments, when each person's are correct—this is surely an extremely tiresome piece of nonsense, if the truth of Protagoras is true, and not merely an oracle speaking in jest from the impenetrable sanctuary of the book."[6] If everything is always in flux and perception is knowledge, then we are always talking past each other and have no way of acknowledging, stabilizing, or building upon common reference points in our interactions with each other.

The key postulate to the Protagorean position that "perception is knowledge," viz., the Heraclitean notion that "everything is in flux," both supports and undercuts Protagorean theory of knowledge. If "everything is in flux," then all we have to go by in validating and constructing an external world are our perceptions from moment to moment. By the same token, however, there is no perception (or series of perceptions) stable enough to be able to sustain the weight of an external world. Heraclitean metaphysics both directs us to assign credence to the notion of "perception" and denudes that conception of any philosophic usefulness.

---

[4] Plato, *Theaetetus,* trans. H. N. Fowler, Loeb Classical Library (Cambridge: Harvard University Press, 1961), 161d.
[5] Ibid., 161d–e.
[6] Ibid., 161e–162a.

We are now in a position to appreciate how the two parts of the *Theaetetus* relate to one another. On the surface, there appears to be an abrupt transition on the dialogue between a discussion of Protagoras and Heraclitus in the first part and a consideration of Parmenides in the second. What underlying currents of thought link the two sections of the dialogue? One possibility is that, after confronting the dead ends that appear pursuant to primacy upon perception, Plato turns to Parmenides as a theorist of the superior alternative of mind-ordained categories.

But there are reflexive dilemmas that arise from an invocation of mind-ordained categories as a source of knowledge. The focus of the second part of the dialogue, personified by Parmenides, is that "knowledge is to be found not in the experiences but in the process of reasoning about them; it is here, seemingly, not in the experiences, that it is possible to grasp being and truth."[7] Socrates adds that "we shall not now look for knowledge in the sense-perception at all, but in whatever we call that activity of the soul when it is busy by itself about the things which are."[8] Theaetetus add that this activity is called "judgment" (in contrast to perception).[9] Socrates then introduces an issue that is central to the argument of the *Cratylus* and drives the argument in the same direction as that pursued in the earlier dialogue, viz., the issue of false judgment. The reflexive dilemma surrounding this issue is that, "if admitted, it would mean that the same man must, at one and the same time, both know and not know the same objects."[10] If what one knows is a judgment, it could not possibly be false. If it is false, it is not—and could never have been—a judgment. What are the logical mechanics of a judgment that is false? How does a string of words manage to support both identities simultaneously?

The *Cratylus* carefully explores this problem. Cratylus asks, "Why, Socrates how can a man say that which is not?—say something and yet say nothing? For is not falsehood saying the thing which is not?"[11] According to Cratylus, the idea of uttering or formulating a falsehood gives rise to a daunting issue of reflexivity. A statement that one designates or acknowledges to be false is both a statement and a nonstatement. In order to identify that which one is ruling out as being false, one needs to utter a string of words which one then goes on to declare or show to be unsustainable. The sentence(s) has (have) to be both viable for identification purposes and unsustainable for argument or truth-affirming purposes. It would appear that, if a sentence lacks adequate truth content, it also lacks that degree of intelligibility and coherence necessary to expose itself as lacking such content. The idea of false statement or sentence appears to be inconsistent, trying to have it both ways: the statement has sufficient logical coherence and autonomy *to be able to be identified* as a statement which is not true.

In order to grapple with the paradoxes of reflexivity, Socrates invokes nominalism. He does this when he asks Theaetetus to formulate an amplified theory of knowledge in the face of the mounting paradoxes affecting the mind-ordained categories position:

---

[7] Ibid., 186d.
[8] Ibid., 187a.
[9] Ibid., 187a.
[10] Ibid., 196b–c.
[11] Socrates, *Cryaltus*, trans. H.N. Fowler, Loeb Classiacal Library (Cambridge: Harvard University Press, 1963), 429d.

Theaetetus: Oh, yes, Socrates, that is just what I once heard a man say; I had forgotten, but now it's coming back to me. He said that it is true judgment with an account that is knowledge; true judgment without an account falls outside of knowledge. And he said that the things of which there is no account are not knowable (yes he actually called them that), while those which have an account are knowable.

Socrates: Very good indeed. Now tell me, how did he distinguish these knowable and unknowables? I want to see if you and I have the same version.

Theaetetus: I don't know if I can find that out; but I think I could follow if someone explained it.

Socrates: Listen then to a dream in return for a dream. In my dream, too, I thought I was listening to people saying that the primary elements, as it were, of which we and everything else are composed, have no accounts. Each of them, in itself, can only be named; it is not possible to say anything else of it, either that it is or that it is not. That would mean that we were adding being or not-being to it; whereas we must not attach anything, if we are to speak of that thing itself alone. Indeed we ought not to apply to it even such words as "as itself" or "that," "each," "alone," or "this," or any other of the many words of this kind; for these go the round and are applied to all things alike, being other than the things to which they are added, whereas if it were possible to express the element itself and it had its own proprietary account, it would have to be expressed without any other thing. As it is, however, it is impossible that any of the primaries should be expressed in an account; it can only be named, for a name is all that it has. But with the things composed of these, it is another matter. Here, just in the same way as the elements themselves are woven together, so their names may be woven together and become an account of something—an account being essentially a complex of names. Thus the elements are unaccountable and unknowable, but they are perceivable, whereas the complexes are both knowable and expressible and can be objects of true judgment.

Now when a man gets a true judgment about something without an account, his soul is in a state of truth as regards that thing, but he does not know it; for someone who cannot give and take an account of a thing is ignorant about it but when he also got an account of it, he is capable of all this and is made perfect in knowledge.[12]

The second, Parmenidean portion of the *Theaetetus* can be read in either of two ways. It can be read first as a broadening of the problem of pursuing a dialectical plan of philosophical exploration that exhibits how issues of reflexivity emerge just as forcefully when one assigns primacy to mind-ordained categories as when one accords primacy to perception. The dialogue can alternatively be read as a delineation of a solution to the problem predicated upon the intermediate role performed by a particular mind-ordained category, viz., nominalism. While the structure and the content of the dialogue as a whole clearly suggest a broadening of the problem, the dialogue also introduces elements that facilitate the inferring of the second approach.

The second part of *Theaetetus* can be treated as a return to the implicit strategy of the *Cratylus*. Nominalism restores consistency to our otherwise aborted statements by invoking circularity for the smallest possible meaning and reference quotients of sentences, which now cannot fail the test of consistency because nominalism facilitates the establishment of a rigid barrier between one small meaning and reference quotient and the next. With regard to the paradoxes attendant to the formulation of the notion of a false judgment, for example, the attribution of falseness has to be nominalistically severed from the articulation of the judgment—with the presupposi-

---

[12] *Theaetetus,* 201d–202c.

tions of statement and utterance in each case closely matching (or duplicating) the logical requisites of sentential coherence. By blocking out contact with and reference to an external world, nominalism enables meaning and reference to be distributed across sentences in a thoroughly insular, circular fashion. This would be an example of Jean-François Lyotard's "suspicion of metanarrativity" enacted on a micro logical-linguistic level. What we need by way of a background assumption to make a particular component of a sentence work is nominalistically supplied. If circularity appeared first under the guise of problem, when we couldn't get our sentences to work unless we read back the fractured results of the requirement of consistency into the presuppositions of the words and phrases needed to compose our sentences, then nominalism provides us with a key to transform circularity into a solution for its own problem by insulating the requirements of sentential consistency and coherence from the constraints exerted by the external world. We can now apportion "assumption" and "presupposition" governed exclusively by the requirements of reflexivity undisturbed by considerations of what the world is supposed to be like.

The *Theaetetus* is unusual among Plato's dialogues for its autobiographical musings. Socrates tried to fix for Theaetetus the nature and limits of his personality. The supreme metaphor that he adopts, and whose ramifications he fully discusses, is that of the midwife:

> Socrates: Then do you mean to say that you have never heard about my being the son of a good and hefty midwife, Phaenarete?
>
> Theaetetus: Oh, yes I've heard that before.
>
> Socrates: And haven't you ever been told that I practice the same art myself?
>
> Theaetetus: No, I certainly haven't.
>
> Socrates: But I do, believe me. Only don't give me away to the rest of the world will you? You see, my friend it is a secret that I have this art. That is not one of the things you hear people saying about me, because they don't know; but they do say that I am a very odd sort of person, always causing people to get into difficulties. You must have heard that surely?
>
> Theatetus: Yes I have.

* * * *

> Socrates: I mean that it is the midwives who can tell better than anyone else whether women are pregnant or not.

* * * *

> Socrates: There's another thing too. Have you noticed this about them, that they are the cleverest of matchmakers, because they are marvelously knowing about the kind of couples whose marriage will produce the best children?

* * * *

> Socrates: So the work of the midwives is a highly important one; but it is not so important as my own performance. And for this reason, that there is not in midwifery the further complication, that the patients are sometimes delivered of phantoms and sometimes of realities and that the two are hard to distinguish. If there were, then the midwife's greatest and noblest function would be to distinguish the true from the false offspring—don't you agree?

Theaetetus: Yes, I do.

Socrates: Now my art of midwifery is like theirs in most respects. The difference is that I attend men and not women, and that I watch over the labor of their souls, not of their bodies. And the most important thing about my art is the ability to apply all possible tests to the offspring, to determine whether the young mind is being delivered of a phantom, that is, an error, or fertile truth. For one thing which I have in common with the ordinary midwives is that I myself am barren of wisdom. The common reproach against me is that I am always asking questions of other people but never express my own views about anything, because there is no wisdom in me; and that is true enough. And the reason of it is this, that God compels me to attend the travail of others, but has forbidden me to procreate. So that I am not in any sense a wise man; I cannot claim as the child of my own soul any discovery worth the name of wisdom. But with those who associate with me it is different. At first some of them may give the impression of being ignorant and stupid; but as time goes on and our association continues, all who God permits are seen to make progress—a progress which is amazing both to other people and to themselves. And yet it is clear that this is not due to anything they have learnt from me; it is that they discover within themselves a multitude of beautiful things, which they bring forth into the light. But it is I, with God's help, who deliver this offspring.

* * * *

There is another point also in which those who associate with me are like women in childbirth. They suffer the pains of labor, and are filled day and night with distress; indeed they suffer far more than women. And this pain my art is able to bring on, and also to allay.[13]

I believe that we are presented in the *Theaetetus* with a central connection that is integral to the design and justification of liberal democracy. Philosophical thought beginning at either end, whether with the particular and perceived or with the general and imposed, eventuates in incoherence. In both cases we are not able to bring our analytical apparatus into harmony with our judgmental and decision-making practices. The gap between how we reason and how we judge can only be closed by assigning a central role to circularity in reshaping our premises in the light of the directions and ends of action we wish to pursue.

Given the limitations of our argumentative condition, the appropriate organization of human life consists in a preoccupation with process. The quintessentialy human moments are associated with movement, with fashioning the new, with giving birth. The common thread running through Socrates' self-description and self-presentation is that his powers are largely defined in negative terms. He is not able to attain truth, but he can perform the much more humble task of helping his interlocutors to distinguish between "phantoms" and "reality." He can point to logical fallacy and expose the weaknesses of arguments even if he cannot arrive at truth. Socrates himself is "barren of wisdom." He can only nudge others to deeper levels of critical awareness and to more refined and self-aware reformulations of their positions. The progress some of his dialogue partners make "is not due to anything they have learnt from" him. He merely gets them to see more clearly who they are and what is already within them. Intellectual growth is a "labor"; it is defined negatively in terms of the losses it

---

[13] Ibid., 149a–151a.

exacts from those devoted to it. The cultivation of "midwifery" is a function of "tongue tiedness" of thought which, in turn, is a function of certain logical and linguistic constraints.

After any beginning wherein we articulate new possibilities, there arise endless deflections, distractions, reconsiderations, and reformulations that restore us to some point in the middle (poised for a new beginning) instead of the end glimpsed at the outset. Since the return to beginnings is everlasting, the definitively philosophical emotion becomes wonder: "This is where philosophy begins and nowhere else."[14] Wonder is preeminently the emotion that defines our attitude toward beginnings. To be in a position to initiate things again and again is a primal source of human wonder.

Plato's argument in the *Theaetetus* lends support to Stuart Hampshire's recent contention: "It would be a gain in clarity to discard the old psychology of separate faculties, with its distinction between reason and imagination, and to substitute for it the contrast between convergent and divergent thought."[15] Plato shows how dominant categories and values adumbrated by reason, for example, "perception," "flux," and "the One," are really devoid of defensible and sustainable content outside the ambit of circular definition. Communities engaging in discourse with Protagorean and Heraclitean biases need to reach convergence among themselves concerning the precise content to be invested in such a term as *immediate knowledge*. "Circularity as solution" then provides us with a formal mapping tool for reinserting the revised content into the original term. The prominence of circularity in Plato's argument challenges us to cultivate a scaled-down conception of reason that is attentive to the ways in which it represents a congealed set of judgment-rendering social practices (convergence), rather than a group of criteria that can be objectively defined, defended, and applied.

The fluid boundaries between reason and imagination throw further light on Socrates' emphasis on *process* in the *Theaetetus*. What is being created anew each time through Socrates' application of his art of "midwifery" is not just a particular person's capacity to refine his argument and become more critically self-aware. It is thought itself that is being recast through Socratic prodding. "Reason" and "imagination" are porous categories that get continually rearticulated in the light of each application of critical reason.

II

Circularity is a central organizing motif in Platonic thought that serves to buttress liberal democratic political categories and values. There are several key examples.

Plato's Theory of Ideas, which relegates the facts of the material world to an inferior ontological status, regarding them as mere copies of eternal Forms, can be construed as a metaphoric and picturesque way of stating that so-called facts are dependent on theory, that the world of theory is underdetermined by the universe of fact. The lack of constraint exerted by facts upon theories suggests that facts borrow at least part of their identity from our theoretical commitments and understanding; what then gets denominated as "facts" has already been influenced and "tainted" by theory.

---

[14] Ibid., 155d–e.
[15] Stuart Hampshire, "Review of *Looking at Giamocetti,* by David Sylvester," *The New York Times Review of Books* XLII (13 July 1995): 48.

If the Theory of Ideas constitutes an encoding of circularity, then we should expect a strong link with "process." Where is the theme of "process" to be found in the *Republic*? One major place to trace it is in an area that is usually taken to represent the prevalence of authoritarian, and even totalitarian, motifs in the *Republic*: the career and the role of philosopher-kings. If these rulers conform to the Socratic model established in the *Theaetetus,* then that which distinguishes them from other members of society is an acute awareness of the limitations of reason which nurtures their cultivation of the Socratic art of midwifery, that is, of devotion to process, to intellectual movement, and to new beginnings. Preoccupation with process comes through at two points the *Republic,* viz., in the course of study that Plato plotted for future philosopher-kings and in the allegory of the cave. At its highest reaches, the philosopher-kings' education consists of training in abstract categories of thought such as mathematics, astronomy, and logic. The analytical payoffs of such an education are richly exemplified in the *Theaetetus* where Socrates underscores again and again how philosophical theories fail to reach their targets, how they fail to account for their ostensible objects and restore us continually to the thick middle of our argumentative condition where only the wonder associated with new beginnings serves to give us a momentary reprieve from our perplexity. The Platonic philosopher molded after the Socrates of the *Theaetetus* is able to challange more effectively than anyone else the possibility of substantive outcomes, theories, and justifications.

Almost after the manner of George Santayana in *The Last Puritan*,[16] Plato's allegory of the cave captures the sense of why, on philosophical grounds, it is misguided to be a philosopher. The philosopher returns to the realm of shadows, to the cave, not just because he seeks to be a public benefactor or because he declines to be ruled by someone inferior to himself, but also and most importantly because his return is a central part of the teaching he has imbibed from the uppermost reaches of his philosophical education. Under the critical, negatively trained eye of the philosophical analyst, most substantive positions in philosophy get deconstructed back into the constellation of aspirations, visions, and partial insights out of which they were composed. Philosophical analysis converts substance back into process. As a way of registering his personal credence in the value and primacy of process, the philosopher returns to the realm of shadows and agrees to take part in the establishment and governing of a state which enshrines the supremacy of process by virtue of his very participation in the tasks of rulership.[17]

Circularity is manifested in many subtle but significant ways in Plato's *Republic* as well as in his other dialogues. Circularity suggests that philosophical arguments don't eventuate in anything. They reflect back to us what we put into them. How, then, does the discourse called philosophy proceed? What points are being made? And how *can* they be made? Two dominant characteristics of Plato's philosophical writing relate to these questions. The first is the proliferation of multiple analogies in Plato's writing. If circularity means that what you theoretically initiate bubbles up with possibilities and then trails off into logical nothingness, then the argumentative thread of philosophical inquiry has to be spread across numerous philosophical ini-

---

[16] George Santayana, *The Last Puritan* (New York: Scribner's, 1935).
[17] Counterexamples to my thesis concerning the values being promoted in the Republic are addressed systematically in my book *Skepticism and Political Participation* (Philadelphia, Pa.: Temple University Press, 1990), 74–84.

tiatives, which, while they don't build cumulatively upon one another, subterraneously trade upon each other's insights and associations. Plato is the philosopher of narrativity *par excellence*, but not primarily a teacher of facticity. For him, what we conceptually articulate defines the *multiple* worlds that we inhabit. Narratives can be built up through quantum leaps and elisions; that is, through mirrorlike reflections on each other's starting points that enable self-contained narratives, metaphors, and analogies to respond to and expand upon and revise each other's initiating impulses without composing or yielding an argument.

Two examples are especially germane. In many of Plato's dialogues, the gods loom as a revealing analogy for the human subject matter under discussion. The gods become a drawing board for a discourse about humanity. In the *Cratylus* Socrates juxtaposes the relationship between words and things to our understanding of the gods. "Saying by way of preface, as I said before of the Gods, that of the truth about them we know nothing and do but entertain human notions about them."[18] Plato's invocation of an abstract theoretical vocabulary to make sense of experience already begins to engender dilemmas of an "unbridgeable" (except through the mechanism of circularity) distancing between words and things. In the passage quoted, Plato projects these dilemmas onto the Greek gods, thereby initiating the process of transforming the secular relationship between words and things from a perspective that calls the transformation itself into question by exposing the human roots that nurtured it.

Platonic circularity is also evident in the "just soul" / "just commonwealth" analogies that are central to the *Republic*. Throughout that dialogue, Plato works with a conception of politics as an omnipresent human phenomenon, one that is not restricted to what takes place in the public sphere. According to Plato, politics does not arise in a determinate historical and social context as a response to a preexisting situation of conflict between men. Instead, it emerges whenever human beings attain to that degree of self-consciousness that allows them to perceive that acting in recognizably human ways nearly always involves the subordination of certain aspects of self to others. Since the very activity of structuring, divorced from historical or social setting, is regarded as a manifestation of the political, of the exertion of power, politics emerges as a kind of primary datum in human experience.

It is possible to define the relationship between the Theory of Ideas, the just soul, and the just commonwealth as a series of conceptual circles reflecting off each other in a state of permanent disequilibrium. From this perspective, the line separating "metaphor" from "reality" becomes shadowy and blurred. The political realm itself can be viewed as the institutionalization of a gigantic "elsewhere." Politics is invented in order to pin down the nature of the human, the personal, and the private. As the largest and most impressive realm of the constructed, it is most revealing of human nature. Or, conversely, the soul as a forum for the application of political, ordering categories such as "justice" is suggestive of the need for the invention—or the periodic reinvention—of the human, and of how ironic and futile that task is. The urge to encompass "reality" with a theory that cannot be incontrovertibly grounded therein suggests that the human will always be a politically chiseled structure despite all of our periodic efforts to rescue it from the political. In our urge to be liberated, we stack the cards against ourselves so that we foreclose further routes toward liberation.

---

[18] *Cratylus,* 425c–d.

Another feature of Plato's philosophical writing that relates to circularity is his choice of the dialogue form. We might say that the dialogue form facilitates the emergence of instant "elsewheres." The introduction by interlocutors of diverse points of view into the speaker's presentation of his theories engenders the proliferation of "circular mirrors" even as the speaker unfolds his ideas. In addition, there are other ways in which dialogue functions as an implicit metaphilosophical commentary on the radical incompleteness of the philosophical enterprise. First, the choice of the dialogue form in which to communicate one's philosophical teaching suggests that philosophy necessarily remains tied to one's presuppositions and assumptions. Even the most elaborately argued philosophical treatise, therefore, has the character of a conversation or dialogue. There is an implicit interrogation hovering over the edges of every philosophical work which helps to articulate and explicate the presuppositions and assumptions out of which the philosophical argument springs.

Second, discourse of whatever sort remains unintelligible without presupposing discourse's relation to silence. What can be quarried from the silence at any given moment in historical time is, to some extent, a function of our networks of interpersonal relationships. What finds its way into discourse is released and sanctioned by those to whom we are relating. All discourse at some pragmatic level is dialogue. Third, in dialogue, language approximates the self-consuming rhythms of silence which overwhelm it. The cutting-in by interlocutors of diverse and unpredictable perspectives is suggestive of the impoverishment of language in the face of what has not yet been put into words. The jagged edges of language that human speech has not yet refined (which is a prominent characteristic of language emerging in the course of conversation) evoke an image of language perpetually on the defensive and unable to adequately protect itself against the destabilizing incursions of the awareness of the unsaid and the unsayable. Finally, time continually destabilizes discourse. What we have just said, at any given moment in time, stands on the brink of dissolving in the face of the onslaught of new sense impressions and internally generated images that are a function of the dispersal of our being over an extended and continuing time frame. Dialogue temporalizes discourse. It projects it as being a function of time. By its very diffraction and fragmentation, dialogue conjures up an image of a beginning that antedates all beginnings, when the convergence of nascent language with experience is preserved without developed language. Issues of reflexivity in philosophy constitute the obdurate traces in the logical spaces of language of this pristine moment in the history of consciousness. The dialogue form, by its very transitory and fragmentary character, evokes the specter of a prelinguistic state in which wholeness is indistinguishable from speechlessness (the absence of language).

III

Tucked away in the argument of the *Theaetetus* are the theoretical seeds of another democratic tradition aside from liberal democracy, viz., participatory democracy. In his exposition of some strands of the Protagorean-Heraclitean position, Socrates says the following:

> Of these [perceptions] we must understand in the same way—as indeed we were saying before—that no one of them *is* anything in itself; all things, of all kinds whatsoever, are coming to be through association with one another, as the result of motion. For even in the case of the active and passive motions it is impossible, as they say, for thought,

taking them singly, to pin them down to being anything. There is no passive till it meets the active, no active except in conjunction with the passive; and what, in conjunction with one thing is active, reveals itself as passive when it falls in with something else.

And so, wherever you turn there is nothing, as we said at the outset, which in itself is just one thing; all things are coming into being relatively to something. The word "to be" must be totally abolished...nor should we allow the use of such words as "something," "of something," or "mine," "this," or "that," or any other name that makes things stand still. We ought, rather, to speak according to nature and refer to things as "becoming," "being produced," "passing away," "changing," ; for if you speak in such a way as to make things stand still, you will easily be refuted. And this applies in speaking both of the individual case and of many aggregated together—such an aggregate, I mean, as people call "man" or "stone," or to which they give the names of different animals and sorts of things.[19]

In this proto-Hegelian passage, Plato wages conceptual warfare on those who mistakenly confuse "becoming" with "being." In the ontology implied by this passage, the only thing that is real is the temporary configuration of relationship, the momentary crystallization of power. Everything beyond that is a misleading reification that deflects human beings away from the reality (realization) of how their humanity is asserted and transformed. Implicit in Socrates' words is a critique of the equation that is central to the argument of the *Theaetetus* taken as a whole. That argument goes from the instability and incoherence of all starting points in philosophy to assigning primacy to process. Promoting the value of process is as compatible with liberal democracy's focus on institutional structure and design as it is neglectful of the power-nurturing potential of individual thoughts and actions. Liberal representative democracy, with its balanced institutional translation of the value of process, develops intimations of the dominant part of the *Theaetetus*. Participatory democracy, however, takes inspiration from the dialogue's secondary argument and emphasizes power and self-empowerment as the authentic loci for human flourishing.

If Hobbes is the premier early modern theorist of translation of the process-oriented, potentially representational teaching of the *Theaetetus,* Machiavelli is the premier early modern theorist of the translation of the *Theaetetus* setting the stage for its later use by participatory democracy theorists. Machiavelli theorizes power in such a way that, the more fully it is displaced, the more effective it becomes. One can trace the origins of this insight to an indirect intertextual relation that subsists between *The Prince* and *The Republic,* as well as to the more direct intertextual relation that is present between *The Prince* and the *Theaetetus*. One could say that an implicit intertextual critique voiced by *The Prince* against *The Republic* is that the inverse relationship between the real and the ideal announced by Plato's Theory of Ideas (with the ideal being more real than any of its actualization's of translations) is not something that characterizes the relationship between the earthly realm and some supersensible realm but properly inheres within the earthly realm itself. Power is present in its most convincing form, the Machiavellian critique implies, when it does not have to be used overtly in order to achieve its intended results. When a reputation for power is sufficient to net a political actor the results he desires, then power is present in its most consummate form. The need to actually resort to power to attain one's ends in politics is symptomatic of the precariousness of one's power. The opti-

---

[19] *Theaetetus,* 156e–157c.

mal state that every political actor should strive for is one in which the ends of power are achieved—people act in conformity with one's wishes—without having to mobilize the costly means of power, which always leads to its further erosion.

According to Machiavelli, therefore, power is a function of nonactions and nonevents. It is rooted in a series of counterfactual circumstances. In order to assess the full range of a political actor's power, according to Machiavelli, it is important to take into account what political goals the actor was able to achieve on the basis of a reputation for power and what pitfalls he was able to avoid because of a strict economizing of means in relation to ends that enabled him to husband power for use of future, more dire occasions. It is what takes place beyond the screen of visible action that is a more reliable indicator of the power of statesmen than statesmen's actions taken by themselves.

The stress on a principle of economy throughout Machiavelli's concrete strategic and tactical advice—tailoring means to make them exactly commensurate with the ends desired—reflects the larger insight that power is always in short supply, to the powerful as well as the powerless. Machiavelli recommends, for example, that the political actor build his relationship with his followers on the basis of fear rather than hatred, which would represent an overshooting of the mark to control and would therefore be counterproductive. The consummate expression of power is its invocation without its direct use. The prescriptive use of civil religion to advance the ends of the state is another example of the same phenomenon in Machiavelli's thought.

A lesson that social-contract theorists learned from Machiaveli is that state-making should consist in minimizing overt uses of power. This insight is institutionalized in classical liberal theory in the imagery and argument of the social contract, where the assertion of power is depicted as a prepolitical, precivil act. What marks the fashioning of civil society is the containment of power in its unbridled, menacing forms.

Machiavelli extends the argument of *Theaetetus*. Power as endless displacement is symptomatic of the foundationless character of reason which suffers displacement by power just as every exercise of power is, or will be, displaced by another. In a liberal democracy, however, our circular argumentative position is redeemed by its institutionalization—a measure that makes for the most economical displays of power and consists in its radical displacement.

The End of the Cold War and the Collapse of Conservative and Liberal Statism

Robert J. Bresler

I

The political legacy of the New Deal and the impact of the cold war kept alive a rationale for a powerful central state. From the late 1930s until the mid–1960s, the American public had a confidence in the federal government and, for that matter, most of our dominant institutions—the universities, the corporations, the churches, and the military. Liberalism was ascendent. It was associated with strong presidents, victory in World War II, early foreign policy successes in the cold war (Marshall Plan, Berlin Blockade, NATO, democratization of Germany and Japan), the broadening of prosperity, new opportunities for workers and minorities and a dramatic increase in the nation's wealth. The New Dealers, who considered themselves the rightful heirs of nineteenth–century populism, appealed to the working man and the rural poor. New Deal liberalism sounded major themes and spawned proposals designed to appeal to a broad base of working middle class Americans—Social Security, protection of unionism, the G.I. Bill of Rights, regional economic development (Tennessee Valley Authority and the Rural Electrification Administration). Although New Deal liberalism attracted intellectuals, it was deeply rooted in grass roots American institutions—unions, the urban machines, and Southern rural communities. The loyalties it gained, it kept for generations.

The first Republican president elected in the era, Dwight Eisenhower, understood the central political reality of his time, viz., that far from fearing government, Americans had developed an appetite for it. Eisenhower's victory over Senator Robert A. Taft, an anti–New Dealer and opponent of Truman's internationalist foreign policy, placed the Republican party solidly in the center of American politics. Consistent with this positioning, the Eisenhower administration developed a consolidationist approach to the welfare state that served to make the New Deal off limits to any serious conservative attack. In 1954, Eisenhower wrote his brother Edgar, who had been critical of his domestic policies, "Should any political party attempt to abolish Social Security, unemployment insurance, and eliminate labor laws and farm programs, you would not hear again of that political party in our political history."[1]

---

[1] Stephen Ambrose, *Eisenhower the President* (New York: Simon and Schuster, 1984), 218–20.

During the Eisenhower years, the Cold War served as the central rationale for the expansion of the state into new areas of domestic life. Supporters of the modest civil rights laws of 1957 and 1960 claimed such legislation would enhance our influence in post–colonial Africa. And fanciful as it may seem today, the Eisenhower administration made the argument that the Interstate Highway Act of 1956 would facilitate the evacuation of our cities in the event of a Soviet nuclear attack. The National Defense Education Act of 1958, which funded new graduate programs, was a direct response to the Soviet's successful launch of the Sputnik satellite and the perception that we were losing our technological edge.

These programs and their accommodation of the state's expansion were at the heart of what Eisenhower called "modern Republicanism." The relatively modest costs of the programs, an expanding economy, and a reduced post–Korean War defense budget allowed Eisenhower to balance the budget and maintain the Republican tradition of fiscal restraint. Nonetheless, this was a smorgasbord of liberalism and conservatism without sharp edges or a clear definition. As political commentator E. J. Dionne put it, "Modern Republicanism was not so much a philosophy as a balancing act."[2] Any serious criticism of the growth of the state was relegated to the political fringes. In fact, such a critique had no major constituency. A broad consensus enveloped American politics: liberals accepted the realities of corporate power and conservatives adjusted to the welfare state. Eisenhower's consensus politics served his presidency well, but it did little for the Republican party except dilute their traditional critique of statism and cloud its vision. Modern Republicanism excited few and had no significant constituency. Two years after Republicans won control of Congress in the 1952 Eisenhower landslide, legislative supremacy reverted to Democrats, who retained it for decades.

The slow growth of the Republican party in the South during the 1950s provided a political base for a new generation of conservatives. With Richard Nixon placing himself out of contention and Nelson Rockefeller embarrassed by his marital complications, Barry Goldwater, the new hero of Republican conservatives, captured the 1964 presidential nomination. But modern Republicans found Goldwater's outside the consensus and his nomination unacceptable. The party was torn asunder, and the 1964 election became a rout for the Republican party.

The 1950s' consensus placed limits on liberalism as well. A conservative coalition consisting of Republicans and Southern Democrats blocked both Harry Truman's Fair Deal and John Kennedy's New Frontier. These programs, despite their different labels, were essentially expansions of the New Deal calling for federal aid to education, public housing, medical insurance, and civil rights.

Lyndon Johnson's landslide victory over Barry Goldwater in 1964 provided massive Democratic majorities in Congress, exceeding those of any election since 1936. A new Congressional majority dominated by northern liberal Democrats overcame the old conservative coalition. With Johnson's prodding, Congress enacted programs far more ambitious than anything Truman or Kennedy had proposed. Ironically, it was in this moment of triumph that the Democratic party began a transformation that was to divorce it from its populist roots.

In his zeal to take advantage of a compliant Congress, Lyndon Johnson designed programs for which there had been no grass–roots demand. His Great Society was the product of an emerging new class of policy intellectuals, that is, carefully selected

---

[2] E. J. Dionne, Jr., *Why Americans Hate Politics* (New York: Simon and Schuster, 1991), 175.

social scientists, lawyers, and social workers. Poverty, they assumed, resulted from behavioral pathologies that could be ameliorated by the right mix of interventionist strategies and government programs. For example, the Jobs Corps would provide remedial programs to make troubled teenagers employable; the Manpower Development program would retrain unemployed workers; Head Start would provide preschool education for poor children; Legal Services would give the poor access to the courts for class–action suits; and the Community Action Program would allow the federal government to contract with community groups to administer local antipoverty programs.

Each program generated a bureaucratic enclave and a Great Society officialdom of highly educated, increasingly well–paid bureaucratic experts. Designed to serve a special constituency of governmental clients, the Great Society made little impact upon the lives of most working and middle class Americans. Even those liberal programs earlier designed to serve broad interests underwent a narrowing of focus as, for example, federal aid to education became a tool for desegregating schools in the South.

Instead of reinforcing working and middle class support, liberal programs alienated those who had been the backbone of liberal majorities. The Community Action Program created elective antipoverty boards and regional offices staffed by political opponents of local Democratic politicians. Model Cities, another Great Society initiative, was, according to political historian Michael Barone, "a social scientist's dream and a mayor's nightmare, in which the resources of all government aid were supposed to be poured into a singled favored neighborhood."[3] If you were neither elderly, poor, nor black, the Great Society was merely something to pay for or read about.

Johnson's conduct of the Vietnam War served to divide his constituency even deeper. Reluctant to withdraw or to escalate the conflict, Johnson and his theater commander, General William Westmoreland, conducted a war of attrition eventually requiring over 500,000 troops against a determined North Vietnamese. With educational deferments available to the sons of the middle and upper class, the war was fought primarily by high school graduates and dropouts.

White working class alienation found its first political expression in the presidential campaigns (1964, 1968, and 1972) of Governor George Wallace (D–Ala.). Wallace's attacks on civil rights laws, liberal Supreme Court decisions, unpatriotic antiwar liberals, and "pointy–headed bureaucrats" attracted support from white working class voters in both the North and the South. His appeal, which was more cultural than economic in a period of substantial growth and prosperity, was a fire–bell in the night for Democrats. It was a clear warning that they were losing their grip on their traditional political base, the white working class.

Disillusioned by the Vietnam War and uninspired by the Great Society, the public's faith in government began to falter. Such faith had been essential to the success of the Democratic party. Thus in the presidential elections that followed Johnson's 1964 triumph, losing liberal Democrats (Hubert Humphrey, George McGovern, Walter Mondale, and Michael Dukakis) failed to attract sufficient support from their party's traditional base.

---

[3] Michael Barone, *Our Country: The Shaping of America from Roosevelt to Reagan* (New York: The Free Press, 1990), 408.

Despite their presidential defeats, Democrats continued to control Congress and determine the domestic agenda long after most Americans had lost faith in governmental solutions. In one of the greatest ironies of recent American politics, government grew almost in *indirect* proportion to the public's confidence in it. As James Q. Wilson observed,

> An era, beginning with the New Deal and the Second World War, in which voters saw a government they admired take on tasks it knew how to perform give way to one in which the citizens watched a government they distrusted take on goals it did not know how to achieve and perform tasks that set one citizen against another.[4]

II

The election of Richard Nixon in 1968 did little to stop the trend described by Wilson. Nixon's overheated conservative rhetoric was intended to fan populist anger against student activists and black militants and to sooth the Goldwater and Wallace voters. Nonetheless, he governed in the Eisenhower tradition. If modern Republicanism was a balancing act, the Nixon experience demonstrated how far the scales had tipped. Confronted with a Democratic Congress driven by an environmental and consumers' agenda, Nixon presided over an elephantine growth of the entitlement and regulatory state.

Regulatory legislation passed during his administration reached a hitherto unexplored aspects of American life. Nixon signed into law the Poison Prevention Packaging Act, the Occupational Safety and Health Act, the Consumer Product Safety Act, the Noise Pollution and Control Act, the Equal Employment Opportunity Act, the Vocational Rehabilitation Act, the Safe Drinking Water Act, and the Hazardous Materials Transportation Act. The pages where federal government's regulations are published tripled during his administration.[5] His own chairman of the Council of Economic Advisers, Herbert Stein, has admitted, "Probably more new regulation was imposed on the economy during the Nixon Administration than any other presidency since the New Deal."[6]

Nixon had neither the ideological interest not the political desire to oppose the torrent of environmental activity unleashed by Earth Day in April, 1970. His 1970 State of the Union Address was a virtual charter of environmentalism. "Clean air, clean water, open spaces," Nixon declared, "these should once again be the birthright of every American." Nixon recommended $10 billion to clean the nation's water supplies. In 1971, he proclaimed the first Earth Week and introduced thirty–six environmental proposals. Most became law—the National Environmental Policy Act (which established the Environmental Protection Agency), the Clean Air Act, the Oil Spill Act, the Noise Control Act, the Clean Water Act, the Ocean Dumping Act, the Coastal Zone Management Act, and other antipollution regulations over pesticides and chemicals. A new dimension of the regulatory state was born.[7]

---

[4] James Q. Wilson, "Reinventing Public Administration," *PS: Political Science and Politics* (December 1994): 669.

[5] Jonathan Rauch, "What Nixon Wrought," *New Republic* (16 May 1994): 31.

[6] Herbert Stein, *Presidential Economics: The Making of Economic Policy from Roosevelt to Reagan and Beyond* (Washington D.C., American Enterprise Institute, 1988), 190.

[7] Joan Hoff, *Nixon Reconsidered* (New York: Basic Books, 1994), 22; and Jonathan Aitken, *Nixon: A Life* (Washington D.C.: Regnery Publishing Inc., 1993), 397–98.

Nixon's environmentalism was tempered by his Republicanism, that is, his "modern Republicanism." According to John Whitaker, his assistant director of the Domestic Council, Nixon had no intention of trying, "to our–clean," Senator Ed Muskie, a potential 1972 Democratic presidential nominee.[8] In a private meeting with Henry Ford II and Lee Iacocca concerning auto emission control, Nixon portrayed himself as a bridge between corporate leadership and the environmental activists and as an opponent of the movement's radicalism. "What they are interested in is destroying the system...I am for the system." On numerous environmental issues Nixon attempted to introduce some notion of costs and benefits to the regulatory policy. It was to no avail. As Herbert Stein lamented, "The juggernaut of environmental regulation proved not to be controllable by the Nixon Administration."[9]

Nixon had no intention of rolling back the Great Society. John Ehrlichman, Nixon's top domestic policy advisor, wrote to Chief of Staff, Bob Haldeman in 1970, "In terms of social programs, e.g., manpower training, anti–poverty, environment, health and education, we are doing as much or more than Johnson or Kennedy." Ehrlichman was not exaggerating. In 1972, Nixon signed a bill granting a 20 percent increase in Social Security benefits. During the eight years of the Nixon–Ford Administrations, entitlement and discretionary domestic spending rose from 9.7 percent of GNP to 15.4 percent.

Concerned that rising unemployment and inflation could endanger his reelection prospects in 1972, Nixon unveiled on 15 August 1971, his new Economic Policy, reminiscent of the wartime economic policies of Roosevelt and Truman. It was the brainchild of Treasury Secretary John Connally, former Democratic Governor of Texas and protégé of Lyndon Johnson. Connally convinced Nixon that he needed to make a grand gesture in economic policy in the tradition of Roosevelt and Johnson. Thus, Nixon announced a ninety–day freeze on wages and prices to be administered by a pay board, a price board, and a cost-of-living council, and the suspension of the convertability of foreign-held dollars into gold, allowing the dollar to "float" on international markets. Effective in the short run, the controls produced low inflation and unemployment in 1972 and no doubt assisted in Nixon's landslide victory over George McGovern. Over time, however, they proved to be a tar baby. The Nixon administration was afraid to abandon them, fearing that doing so would unleash another round of inflation. They continued in one form or another until April of 1974. By that time, the Watergate scandals revealed that Nixon had shed whatever inhibitions he may have earlier harbored about the use of government power.

Jimmy Carter approached the presidency as a chastened liberal without an overarching agenda and the dramatic label that would have gone with it. In the 1976 Democratic primaries he presented himself as something of a populist focusing on the problems of unemployment and inflation while minimizing the more diverse social issues. He sounded what later became known as neoliberal themes, that is, reorganizing of government, reducing the bureaucracy, reforming the tax code, and balancing the budget. His approach initially showed promise. In the Florida primary, he attracted enough white working class and black voters to defeat George Wallace; in the Pennsylvania primary Carter defeated labor's candidate, Senator Henry Jackson and the liberal favorite Representative Morris Udall. But Carter soon learned that the

---

[8] Quoted in Hoff, *Nixon Reconsidered*, 23.
[9] Stein, *Presidential Economics*, 195.

limits of how far neoliberalism could carry him with the constituent base of the Democratic party. In order to secure nomination, he had made very costly promises: to the National Education Association that he would support a new Department of Education; to the United Auto Workers that he would introduce a government-sponsored health care plan; and to the Democratic mayors that he would provide them fiscal relief, an urban economic development initiative, and public works jobs.[10] Carter was barely able to keep his black/white populist constituency together in defeating Gerald Ford that November. Carter carried the vast majority of Southern Wallace voters and carried all the Southern states, save Virginia and Florida.

Once in office, Carter could not reconcile his neoliberalism with the demands of the liberal Democrats. The welfare reform proposals that came to his desk from Health, Education, and Welfare Secretary Joseph Califano and Labor Secretary Ray Marshall involved more federal spending for jobs or cash assistance; the recommendation of Housing and Urban Development Secretary Patricia Harris for a national urban policy called for adding another $8 to $12 billion to the $50 billion of aid to cities the government was already spending.[11] In both cases, Carter rejected the proposals. He could develop neither a welfare policy nor an urban policy that pleased core Democratic constituency.

When faced with double-digit inflation in 1979–80, Carter reverted to budgetary austerity that further eroded his support in the party. His fiscal year 1979 budget called for virtually no increase in discretionary domestic spending. Other problems—the Soviet invasion of Afghanistan, the spike oil price, the Tehran hostage crisis, and the rise in interest rates—beset Carter to make his position untenable in 1980. With calamitous events compounding Carter's more fundamental political failure, he could satisfy neither those Americans who were increasingly disenchanted with government nor the poor and the minorities who were convinced that more government spending was essential to their needs. This was a dilemma that no Democratic president could easily resolve.

Carter's inability to connect with the populist base he had tapped in 1976 was symptomatic of the changing public perception of American liberalism. New Deal liberalism was associated with dominant presidents, a great military victory, early cold war foreign policy successes, the broadening of prosperity, new opportunities for workers and minorities, and the dramatic increase in wealth. Post–New Deal liberalism found its dismal associations with military defeat in Vietnam, double–digit inflation, campus unrest, oil shocks, racial quotas, and ineffective presidents. Ted Kennedy's unsuccessful challenge to Carter in the 1980 Democratic primary was additional evidence of how difficult it was to stoke up the old fires.

Ronald Reagan, elected to the presidency with substantial working class support, was the first president of the post World War II era to challenge domestic liberalism and sense its weakness. Reagan realized that working class and middle income Americans no longer equated their economic interests with the growth of the state. In fact, much of their anger was directed at the state and its elites. Reagan's promise of lower taxes, reduced spending, and fewer regulations struck a responsive chord.

---

[10] Stuart E. Eizenstat, "President Carter, the Democratic Party, and the Making of Domestic Policy," in *The Presidency and Domestic Policies of Jimmy Carter*, ed. Herbert D. Rosenbaum and Alexej Ugrinsly (Westport, Conn.: Greenwood Press, 1994), 7.
[11] Burton I. Kaufman, *The Presidency of James Earl Carter* (Lawrence: University Press of Kansas, 1993) 52–54, 74–75.

The results of his administration were mixed. His success in lowering marginal income tax rates was offset by substantial increases in the Social Security tax. Consequently, marginal income tax rates on median income actually rose between 1981 and 1984.[12] Reagan made no effort, after a halfhearted attempt in 1981, to reduce the growth of the entitlement state or discretionary domestic spending. The only programs he succeeded in eliminating were Revenue Sharing and the Comprehensive Education and Training Act (CETA). The latter was replaced by the Jobs and Partnership Training Act.

Reagan favored an activist government in foreign affairs. In order to regain the foreign policy initiative and roll back Soviet influence, he demanded a substantial increase in the defense budget, an expansion of CIA activities in Afghanistan, Angola, and Nicaragua, and the Strategic Defense Initiative to challenge the logic of deterrence. The Iran–Contra affair demonstrated how determined he was to maintain control of foreign policy in the White House and keep it away from Congressional scrutiny. Although Reagan was far more conservative and populist than his centrist Republican predecessors (and successor), he was ideologically attached to the activist government in foreign policy and politically unable to oppose it in domestic policy.

In effect, the cold war muted the populist impulse as much as it clouded conservative government. White middle class anger—directed against international elites in the McCarthy era, civil rights militants and student activists in the 1960s and 1970s, and the media elite in the 1980s and 1990s—served Republican interests in presidential elections. Even so, the politics of Nixon and Reagan did little to build an electoral base with these voters at the congressional, state, or local level. Republican presidents pursued statist policies embellished with populist rhetoric. Nixon helped to institutionalize affirmative action with set–asides and other race-conscious policies; and Reagan gave little active support to the pro–life movement, allowed affirmative action policies to stand, and rarely mentioned school prayer.

The Congressional base of the Republican party remained in the business community whose lobbyists had little on their agenda beyond constituent needs. Most Republicans in Congress settled comfortably into a minority posture, especially in the House, and made no concerted effort to challenge the Democratic majority. For a brief period in the early Reagan years, they built an effective coalition with the Boll Weevil Democrats in order to lower marginal tax rates. In general, they played the politics of pork and constituent service with little hope of ever becoming the majority. As a recent study of House Republicans suggests, many members placed near–term individual interests over party issues, for example, trading votes with Democrats, winning pork–barrel projects, and advancing pet causes.[13] They rarely faced serious opposition at home. Hence, the white working class support for Nixon and Reagan never penetrated far below the presidential level. The Republican party had neither the program nor the grass roots organization to take advantage of it.

The Republican party in the cold war years faced the worst of two worlds—an elitist funding base (Wall Street and business PACs) and a narrow constituent base (small town/rural American and the affluent suburbs). Particularly because the latter base was insufficiently broad, the Republican party's successes were superficial. The

---

[12] David Frum, *Dead Right* (New Republic Books, 1994), 37.
[13] William F. Connelly, Jr. and John J. Pitney, *Congress' Permanent Minority: Republicans in the House* (Lanham, Md.: Littlefield Adams Quality Paperbacks, 1994), 4.

election of Eisenhower was not a broad mandate, but rather a reaction to Democratic failure in Vietnam. Neither victory hastened a political realignment beyond the presidential level. Reagan's victory went somewhat deeper than Eisenhower's or Nixon's and evidenced the potential of the right to capture the white lower- and middle–income vote. But support for Republicans from this direction waned with the end of the 1980s' boom and retirement of Reagan. George Bush, with his preppie manner and upper–class background combined with his themeless domestic program, had little to communicate to the Reagan Democrats. As a surprise to no one, they deserted him for Perot and Clinton in 1992.

The failure of the Republican party to become a voice of populism was, thus, stymied by four ineluctable factors: (1) the imperatives of the cold war viz., a strong central state, high taxes, and an internationalist/interventionist foreign policy; (2) a docile congressional minority satisfied with the politics of pork and constituent service; (3) defensive presidents unable to prevent the growth of interest group liberalism; and (4) a political base dependent upon business money and suburban volunteers. Modern populism's themes of local control, traditional morality, disdain of elites, and isolationism could not be woven into the policies and the politics of cold war Republicanism. In fact, Republicans only played a variation on the theme of cold war liberalism. The seemingly immutable fact of Soviet/American rivalry had created a climate conducive to elitist government and centralized power.

III

The Republican party, despite its failures, demonstrated some potential for building a new populist base. Democrats, on the other hand, seemed at an intellectual dead end. Could the anxieties of many Americans be satisfied by the continued growth of the welfare state?

Ironically, it was the young leaders of the New Left who in the early 1960s saw that the alienation of ordinary people from government would burgeon as a theme in the second half of the twentieth century. In the Port Huron Statement, written in 1962, they declared that "the individual [should] share in those social decisions determining the quality and direction of his life and society [should] be organized to encourage independence in men and provide media for their common participation." As the New Left drifted into counterculture politics, romanticized violence, and vulgar Marxism, it lost an opportunity to reinvigorate liberalism and connect it with working class populism.

The scattered protests of the left on behalf of, for example, peace and/or a nuclear freeze, black activism, feminism, environmentalism, abortion rights, and gay rights, never merged into a coherent movement . More important, their tone and direction had not even the vaguest resemblance to populism. Battles over women's rights, the environment, abortion, the defense budget, and gay rights were removed from much of what was happening in the lives of ordinary people. Of concern to mainstream America were the loss of manufacturing jobs, the deterioration of family life, and the destruction of neighborhoods by drugs and crime.

Disunity of the left was mirrored in the camp of interest group liberalism where a mélange of environmental, consumerism, and affirmative action programs held sway. Although these programs had disparate goals, they had the joint effect of spawning new bureaucracies—for example, the Equal Employment Opportunities Commission, the Environmental Protection Agency, the Occupational Safety and Health Administration, the Consumer Product Safety Commission, and the Civil Rights Division of the Justice Department—that many working class Americans associated with elitism. Affirmative action programs, in contrast to the pro–union New Deal legislation, made white males the target rather than the beneficiary. Environmentalists often placed the protection of wilderness and endangered species over that of working people. As environmental groups such as the National Resources Defense Fund, the Sierra Club, and the National Audubon Society experienced a vast increase in membership, the image of their lobbyists as abstemious Ralph Naders living modestly in Washington and battling for the people was exposed as a myth. For example, in 1991, the president of the National Wildlife Federation administered a budget of $77 million and drew $300,000 in compensation.[14] Despite their public interest rhetoric, many of these groups seemed to fit the special interest mold, asking for resources to be diverted to their cause over others, for example, environmental restrictions versus highway spending.

On many issues, liberals feared populist anger and sought relief in the courts. It was there and not at ballot boxes that liberalism won some of its most important battles over abortion, prayers in school, racial gerrymandering, defendant's rights, censorship of pornography, and affirmative action. Liberals' failure to fight successfully for these causes in the political arena only weakened their public support and reinforced their growing elitist image.

Liberals in the 1970s and 1980s also succeeded in penetrating institutions far removed from the daily lives of working and middle class America, for example, the established foundations, the national media, and higher education. The universities witnessed an explosion of a left–driven agenda for multiculturalism, ethnic studies, women's studies, gay studies, post–modernism, and diversity requirements. These changes at the universities dramatized the gap between the left liberals and middle America whose students desperately needed skills demanded by the marketplace. Many colleges and universities, dominated by a tenured faculty whose mind–set was shaped by the 1960s, had little appreciation of the uncertainties of the marketplace and, thus, supported a curriculum driven by university politics rather than student needs. By the 1990s, higher education was facing a crisis of public confidence, a fact underscored by a steady decline in state funding. No one should be surprised that many parents (particularly working fathers) were reluctant to go deep into debt to expose their children to an increasingly politicized curriculum in which their wars, their history, and their political status were subject to a sustained attack.

The media, the bane of Franklin Roosevelt and Harry Truman and dominated by such conservative publishers as Henry Luce, Colonel Robert McCormick, David Lawrence, and William Randolph Hearst, dramatically transformed itself. Such previously moderate to conservative national news publications as *Time, Newsweek, U.S. News and World Report,* and the *New York Times* became outlets for political and cultural liberalism. The growth of talk radio in the 1990s and the phenomenon of Rush Limbaugh are nothing more than the invention of a national conservative outlet. Ironically, the liberal slant of the media did not have the desired effect of shaping the American mind, but served only to anger ordinary Americans who saw millionaire celebrity journalists as part of a new elite. This elite, concentrated in New York, Los

---

[14] Jonathan Rauch, *Demosclerosis: The Silent Killer of American Government* (Times Books, 1994), 45.

Angeles, Washington, D.C., and universities and colleges towns across America, was far removed from the lives of middle America. Liberals enjoyed a vantage point not for looking at America, but rather for looking down on America.

Given the great influence of the national media on everyday living, middle America's continuing hostility toward them makes the question of their control and bias so explosive. Asked in a *Times–Mirror* survey taken in early 1994, what institution was the most important, 43 percent of respondents cited the media and 22 percent cited Washington. Thus, the more people felt bombarded with messages from the media trashing organized religion and the two–parent family (where as Charles Krauthammer notes, the more their anger heated).

Liberalism increasingly ignored the concerns of ordinary Americans at a time when their economic conditions were deteriorating. Corporate downsizing, stagnant wages, the need for two-earner families, weak unions, and periodic bouts of recession and inflation pinched their lives. Evangelical Christianity grew as a political force. It articulated the revolt against moral upheaval, repugnance of the dominant culture, fear of family deterioration, and the sense of social isolation. If nothing else, evangelical Christianity represents a desire for some certainty and security in a world where the ground is shifting under the feet of so many. And as demonstrated in the recent election, its leaders are politically savvy and well–organized at the grass roots. It is difficult to imagine a new populist movement of any substance without them.

White populist anger was also manifest in many Midwestern and Western referenda votes for term limits and against gay rights and immigration. The 1994 election was an earthquake that will transform the political landscape. Will it result in a political realignment such as those that occurred in 1860, 1896, and 1932 and establish a new governing majority and a new political culture; or does it augur a political dealignment, leaving the political system in disarray and barely governable?

In the 1994 election, the Congressional Republican party became the vehicle and the beneficiary of this anger—white males voted 62 percent Republican, a gain of 11 percent over the 1992 congressional election; white born-again Christians voted 76 percent Republican, a gain of 10 percent; high school graduates voted 52 percent Republican, a gain of 11 percent over 1992; whites in the South voted 65 percent Republican, a gain of 12 percent over 1992. Democrats in turn showed strength among blacks, Jews, gays, liberals, unmarried women (which is where the real gender gap shows up), and people with postgraduate education.

Whereas the populism of the late nineteenth century placed its faith in government action, the populism of the late twentieth century has only disdain for government and little faith in its ability to solve the people's problems.[15] During the Cold War, a combination of patriotism and anticommunism persuaded many working people that a strong central state was necessary. It was needed not only to provide for the common defense but to build highways, educate students, and maintain a degree of ideological control. The end of the Cold War, thought by many to bring about the unhinging of conservatism, may instead be its liberation. Conservatism's attachment to the national security state made it difficult for conservatives to launch a massive attack on bureaucratic centralism. Although it is difficult to imagine conservatives not being in

---

[15] In 1954 only 16 percent of Americans believed that big government was our greatest problem. Recent polls show that the figure is now between 70 and 75 percent. Cited in Michael Vlahos, "The New Wave," *National Review* (26 September 1994), 44.

favor of a strong military in defense of vital national interest, their definition of what constitutes those interests and what threatens them has undergone a major transformation. During the Cold War, many conservatives found their anticommunism more powerful than their isolationism. Cold War anticommunism, rather than being the glue of conservatism, gave it a decidedly ambivalent vision of the state.

Conservative nationalists who opposed Wilsonian nationalism until Pearl Harbor found their instincts reawakened by the muddled neo–Wilsonianism of the Clinton Administration. Rightist opposition to GATT and NAFTA, clearly populist in nature, was stirred not just by economic insecurity but also by fear of the supranational bureaucracies that these agreements have produced. Can Republicans develop a coherent foreign policy, based upon neo–realist principles that avoid the romanticism of isolationism and Wilsonianism? Will a globalized economy make us more interventionist or less? If the answer is in the former, will isolationism metamorphose into economic nationalism with all its potential for populist appeal?

The Wall Street/country club funding base of the Republican party saw the state as a source of largesse, in the form of tax loopholes, subsides, and regulatory favoritism. Although the Eisenhower, Nixon, and Bush administrations had waxed powerful through the bestowal of such gifts, the possibility that this style of governance will continue infuriates most Americans.

Populist anger will be even more white–hot if its political beneficiaries betray it. Should the new Republican Congress produce another construct of timid centrism and interest–group conservatism deferential to business, the next political storm will be even more ferocious.

A populist revolt that substitutes one elite for another without effecting any significant change in the lives of people could become the seedbed of a new authoritarianism. The most disturbing question is whether the social upheaval that so disturbs many Americans—rising crime, family deterioration, job insecurity—can be altered by any set of social policies. Will limited, more decentralized government result in more job security, stronger families, less crime, and reduced drug usage? The globalization of the economy, the information revolution, and the alteration of sexual and social more cannot be wished or legislated away. Riding the tide of populist anger is like riding a tiger; either master it or it will eat you.

Should the Republicans fail, it is unlikely that the already discredited Democrats would benefit. More likely, a new political movement would emerge from the ashes. Its authoritarianism might be pervasive and harsh. Who knows what rough beast will come slouching toward our Jerusalem?

The Vryheid Front on South Africa's Constitution

Chris Woltermann

The apartheid that ended with South Africa's first all–race elections in April of 1994 bore little resemblance to apartheid as it originated among Afrikaner intellectuals before their National party came to power in 1948. Often not differentiated, apartheid's historical and intellectual strains endure as signposts to political commitment in the new South Africa.

Virtually all nonwhites and a majority of whites oppose both kinds of apartheid. Among white opponents, members of the now nonracial National Party occupy the most ironic position in South African politics. Although the party preserves its predecessor's name, its repudiation of apartheid allows such leading Nationalists as F. W. de Klerk and Roelf Meyer to serve President Nelson Mandella, the old party's African National Congress nemesis, as, respectively, his second Executive Deputy President and Minister of Provincial Affairs and of Constitutional Development.[1]

Apartheid's supporters, who may comprise as much as a third of whites, back the Conservative party (now effectively indistinguishable from the Afrikaner Volksfront), the Vryheid Front (or Freedom Front, not to be confused with the newly defunct Freedom Alliance), and/or various paramilitary groups, for example, the Afrikaner Weerstandsbeweging. The Conservatives' and the paramilitarists' adherence to historical apartheid is a major reason why they are fading into oblivion. Other factors are their boycott of the April elections and, for the paramilitarists, their bungled attempt a month earlier to forcibly uphold the Bophuthatswana "homeland" government of Lucas Mangope. Continuing defections from the reactionary right have made the Vryheid Front, registered by General (ret.) Constand Viljoen in early March to contest the April elections, the chief proponent of apartheid, that is, the intellectual's ideal of apartheid. Having received only 2.2 percent of the vote for the National Assembly, the Vryheid Front nevertheless ranked fourth among participating parties. Its program offers the best prospect for South Africa to avoid becoming, as the pre-

---

[1] Meyer's responsibilities have recently grown to include the portfolio of Local Government, as reported by *The Star* (Johannesburg, 26 May 1994), and noted, with attribution to *The Star,* in *South Africa News Update* 22 (1994): 2. Various issues of *South African News Update,* a weekly survey of the South African Press prepared by the South African Consulate General in Chicago, are the source for this paper's statements of fact for the period March through June, 1994.

election rapprochement between the National party and the African National Congress portends to make it, the sort of highly centralized and bureaucratized welfare state that, everywhere in the West, arouses increasing citizen resentment.

Analyzing the Vryheid Front's program is difficult because Viljoen and other party leaders kept their campaign statements sufficiently general to avoid undermining their subsequent position in negotiations with the expected winners of the National Assembly vote, the African National Congress, and the National Party. The latter parties, having indeed received 62.6 percent and 20.4 percent, respectively, of ballots cast, joined with the Vryheid Front and are now engaging in informal negotiations. According to the Vryheid Front's one–page election manifesto, its fundamental objective is a confederal South Africa. The litmus test for such a new order is the establishment of an Afrikaner *volkstaat* (literally, "people's state") enjoying sovereign powers. This option should also be available, the Vryheid Front contends, to every other ethnic group desiring self–determination. The Vryheid Front has not gone public with details on how an Afrikaner volkstaat is to be established, or where and of what size it is to be. Regarding the former consideration, Villjoen is on record as favoring, at least for the time being, negotiations and other peaceful means. Regarding an Afrikaner volkstaat's location and size, the best indicator of the Vryheid Front's intentions is Viljoen's vilification by the Afrikaner Weerstandsbeweging's Eugene Terre'blanche and various Conservatives. These reactionaries have never given up the chimera of preserving (or re–creating, in the contemporary situation) all or most of the old white South Africa, 87 percent of the country's territory. By contrast, the Vryheid Front's territorial ambitions are more modest, albeit still indeterminate.

The Vryheid Front does not openly advocate apartheid, at least by name. Even so, the communitarian emphasis of Viljoen and his supporters should be understood by reference to the philosophy of apartheid dating from the 1940s. Cynics who interpret that philosophy as a rationalization for racial oppression face overwhelming evidence to the contrary. Most supporters of historical apartheid have always accepted the principle that if blacks reside permanently in white–governed territory, they must be enfranchised on a common electoral roll to the detriment of exclusively white governance.[2] The fulfillment of the conditional element in this principle, to the consternation of all but the most stubborn utopians, moved the government in 1986, when the old National Party with its membership restricted to whites ruled the country, to restore South African citizenship to resident blacks who has lost it when their "homelands" had received internationally unrecognized independence. Marking the beginning of the end of historical apartheid, this restoration of citizenship also manifested the abiding influence of apartheid principle on apartheid practice. But, despite the importance of the assumed relation between residency and voting rights, the philosophers of apartheid held still more fundamental principles. These offer the best clue to the Vryheid Front's program.

Although an excellent scholarly discussion of philosophical apartheid is available,[3] a politically motivated explanation by Nicolaas J. Diederichs is more incisive. Diederichs, an early theorist of apartheid and a member of parliament for the old National Party, spoke during parliamentary debate in 1948 of "two outlooks on life, fundamentally so divergent that a compromise is entirely unthinkable." One outlook,

---

[2] Howard Brotz, *The Politics of South Africa* (London: Oxford University Press, 1977).
[3] A. James Gregor, *Contemporary Radical Ideologies* (New York: Random House, 1968), 221–76.

which came to be known as apartheid, Diederichs called "nationalism"; the other was liberalism. Diederichs elaborated:

> On one hand, we have nationalism which believes in the existence...of distinct peoples, distinct languages, nations, and cultures, and which regards the fact of the existence of these peoples and cultures as the basis of its conduct. On the other hand we have liberalism, and the basis of its political struggle is the individual with his so-called rights and liberties.[4]

Here appears explicitly or implicitly everything essential to philosophical apartheid. Conceived in opposition to liberalism, it calls for a polity whose coherence depends on monoculturally-based comity and fellowship among citizens and not on statutory law. A multicultural polity is undesirable because, with the accession of "aliens" to people who interact customarily, laws must be formulated so that members of different cultures can know how to behave in the presence of—and what to expect from—persons different from themselves. Apartheid's monoculturalism entails the ideal of governance as merely cajolery, rule by persuasion, to secure for the governed the benefits of *voluntary* cooperation throughout society.[5] Such governance is, broadly speaking, federal (or confederal) and populist; it assumes that "really existing" people, acting in greater or lesser numbers as circumstances require, should and will do for themselves rather than as government orders them.

Nothing in philosophical apartheid's communitarian rudiments suggest, let alone necessitates, the horrors of historical apartheid. Yet, these began to appear from the inception of the old National Party's rule, e.g., the pro-apartheid milestones as the Prohibition of Mixed Marriages Act (1949) and the Group Areas Act (1950). What happened? In brief, the intellectuals made two mistakes. First, they reflected too little on achieving a monocultural polity from within a multiculturally populated territory; their sophistication concerning how a monocultural polity changes with the entry of foreigners degenerated into muddled naiveté, and comparable political praxis, when they failed to appreciate that they came to power in a markedly unitary South Africa which, as such, was incongruous with their penchant for consensual, implicitly federal politics. Viljoen and his supporters will have to rectify both mistakes if the Vryheid Front's unadmittedly neo-apartheid agenda is to have any chance of ushering in an Afrikaner volkstaat.

Surmounting the second mistake comes down to recognizing that 1994's political realities are not those of 1948. Although the current interim constitution perpetuates—and disguised with a federal veneer—South Africa's heritage, uninterrupted since 1910, as a unitary state, the new universal franchise effectively precludes seces-

---

[4] Quoted by Brotz, *The Politics of South Africa*, 137.
[5] Governance by cajolery, a strange notion even for many social scientists, was nonetheless the norm in the old Boer republics, the Orange Free State, and the Transvaal. The example of Paul Kruger's Transvaal presidency has held particular appeal for Afrikaners ever since the nineteenth century. Poulteney Bigelow described Kruger this way: "He is President among his burghers by the same title that he is elder in his church. He makes no pretense to rule them by invoking the law, but he does rule them by reasoning with them until they yield to his superiority in argument. He rules among free burghers because he knows them well and they know him well. There is no red tape, nor pigeonholes." Quoted by Stuart Cloete, *Against These Three: A Biography of Paul Kruger, Cecil Rhodes, and Lobengula, Last King of the Metabele* (Cambridge, Mass.: The Riverside Press, 1945), 154.

sionist–minded whites from winning power at the polls. Therefore, and in keeping with philosophical apartheid's consensual orientation, the Vryheid Front will be able to secure an Afrikaner volkstaat only by persuading a black–dominated government and, ultimately, black voters to permit it. This is not as farfetched as it may seem; General Viljoen and President Mandela enjoy a relationship of mutual respect. On 2 June 1994, Mandela spoke approvingly, albeit very tentatively, of a possible referendum among Afrikaners to decide upon seeking a South African "homeland." Such an entity, the Vryheid Front's volkstaat, Mandela personally believes would be unfeasible. From the Afrikaner's minority status everywhere in South Africa, it seems that a special territory for them would have to be too small to be meaningful or dependent for its success on either the evacuation of non–Afrikaners from it or their equally unacceptable relegation to second–class status in its politics. Of course, Viljoen is uninterested in a tiny, marginal volkstaat. Thus, negotiations between the Vryheid Front and Mandela's government will necessarily center upon the question, which led the early theorists of apartheid into their first mistake, of how to achieve a monocultural polity from within a multiculturally populated territory.

Every word uttered by the Vryheid Front's negotiators will be wasted effort unless they admit that an Afrikaner volkstaat would have to include more non–Afrikaners than Afrikaners. Far from conceding the case for a volkstaat, this admission would bring a necessary element of realism into the negotiations. An immediate consequence would be that the Vryheid Front would have to jettison the principle, shared by liberalism and philosophical apartheid, that permanent residency establishes entitlement to the franchise. The key to rejecting this principle is the proposition: representation *in* government differs from representation *to* government. Being represented to government can be a reliable method for securing one's liberties. Thus, non–Afrikaners need not feel discomfited by residing in an Afrikaner–run volkstaat provided that they are adequately represented to the Afrikaner's government.

The distinction between "representation in" and "representation to" requires further comment.[6] At issue is where the representative function is fulfilled. Representation in provides a voice within the apparatus of government; representation to can influence government from without. History offers numerous examples of the efficacy of institutionalized representation to government. Roman tribunes could, on behalf of the plebs whom they represented, check injurious legislative and judicial decisions. More recently, classical British Whig liberals insisted on parliamentary representation, not to participate in the king's government but to protect themselves from it. The modern notion of political "participation" stands in diametrical contrast to historical representation in government. Accordingly, two modern intellectuals Emmanuel–Joseph Sieyes and V. I. Lenin, the authoritarian ramifications of their respective participatory systems, Jacobin democracy and Bolshevik democratic centralism. And, in today's Western democracies, growing political "participation" goes hand in glove with the subjection of citizens to the increasingly intrusive, and typically unfunded, mandates of government bureaucrats. "Participation," one suspects, is the modern state's miserly recompense to its subjects for their subservience.

---

[6] The following discussion draws its inspiration from: Dennis Hale and Marc Landy, eds., *The Nature of Politics: Selected Essays of Bertrand de Jouvenel* (New York: Schocken Books, 1987); and H. A. Fagan, *Co-existence in South Africa* (Cape Town: Juta & Co., 1963).

Any advocacy of representation to government as a safeguard for non–Afrikaners in an Afrikaner volkstaat will provoke a predictable retort: if representation to government is so beneficial, secessionist–minded Afrikaners should abandon their dream of being represented in their own volkstaat's government; they should resign themselves to being recalcitrant "outsiders" represented to the new South Africa's multicultural government. *Mutatis mutandis,* this argument is tantamount to that which apologists for historical apartheid formerly employed in futile attempts to persuade blacks to accept whites–only rule. Both arguments are fallacious in that they assume that representation to government can properly function in the context of a large, culturally diverse, modern, and unitary state. To the contrary, given the parameters of size, cultural diversity, and modernity, representation to government requires either a federal or, better yet, insofar as extreme decentralization is implied, a confederal political order.

The South Africa confederation rather nebulously proposed by the Vryheid Front's election manifest would comprise several volkstaats of moderate size and a large, officially nonethnic state. No less sovereign than the latter, each volkstaat would restrict representation in its government to a single cultural/ethnic group. The many persons thereby excluded *de jure* from representation in the various volkstaat governments would parallel the persons excluded *de facto* from the government of the rest of South Africa. Although that black–dominated government would afford representation in it to all, and although it might operate as a liberal democracy and practice the "politics of inclusion," it would exclude residents psychologically incapable of "participating." Such persons, alienated by the prospect of having a merely marginal voice in government by grace of their rulers' condescension, could take solace from, and take up residence within, the appropriate volkstaats established in areas where supporters are already present in considerable numbers. Over time, voluntary migrations might make every state more homogeneous. In the crucial meantime, persons not represented in the government ruling the territory wherein they reside would have ample opportunity for representing their interests—and having their interests represented—to "their" government. Their representation would not be a matter of law, much less of an overarching bill of rights enforced by a unitary shadow–state in mockery of the confederation of sovereign states. The representation at issue would be a practical matter, with the intragovernmentally unrepresented pressuring "their" government through: (1) purely internal ad hoc and institutional means of their own making; (2) the transfer or threatened transfer of their capital and/or labor to another state(s); and (3) the use of government-to-government resources by another state(s) on their behalf. A confederation "structured" along these lines would be a convoluted tangle of accommodations and tensions, a nightmare to anyone fond of neat and orderly constitutionalism, but perhaps the best "system" for South Africans.

A neo–apartheid South Africa as envisioned by the Vryheid Front would also be a neo–liberal South Africa. As such, it would be superior to today's liberal South African unitary state with its federal overlay. Liberalism is problematic because it produces illiberal effects in proportion to how ambitiously it expands the scope of protected individual rights.[7] Oblivious to the theoretical and historical evidence in this regard,

---

[7] Ferdinand Tönnies, an ardent liberal, had no illusions in this respect: "Arbitrary freedom (of the individual) and arbitrary despotism (of the Caesar or the State) are not mutually exclusive. They are only a dual phenomenon of the same situation. They may struggle with each other more or less, but by nature they are allies." Ferdinand Tönnies, *Community & Society,* trans. J. F. Huntington (Indianapolis, Ind.: Liberty Fund, 1993), 187.

South Africa's new constitution makes illiberal governance virtually inevitable. Not only does the constitution appeal to a sweeping and almost visceral individualism. Its provisions to combat discrimination—on the bases of race, gender, sexual orientation, ethnic or social origin, color, age, disability, religion, conscience, belief, culture, and language—read like a parody of contemporary American liberalism at its most aggressive. Requiring 200 pages, the constitution is a dream come true for activist legislators and bureaucrats. They can be expected to prove themselves no less adept than their American counterparts at "benevolently" regulating the minutiae of daily life, thereby reducing personal liberty and social processes of meaningful self-governance to empty posturing.

Movement toward such a statist future is already well underway.[8] The trend will continue unless and until it is derailed, as seems quite likely, by civil war or the emergence of dictatorial government meant to contain tensions threatening civil war. South Africans are at risk because many of them, especially Afrikaners, Cape Coloreds, and Zulus, have not progressed nearly as far as Americans and West Europeans in acquiring habits of subservience to the therapeutic liberal state. South Africans who resist this model are typically African. A proud, populist resistance to the realities of liberal democracy has been the most salient fact in the politics of sub-Saharan ever since decolonization. Spread over thirty-odd states, black Africans have suffered no shortage of liberal democratic constitutions designed to replicate Western political institutions in African contexts. These constitutions engendered powerful governments—more powerful than the erstwhile colonial administrations—that soon made Africans resentful of statist intrusions into their lives. The upshot having civil wars and/or dictatorial regimes, black Africans compiled a record of nearly unrelieved failure in their efforts to build sustainable institutions of benign governance. All the preconditions and otherwise, for adding another chapter to this sorry history are already available in South Africa.

The much-heralded "new South Africa" may to turn into a lamentable disaster, and it is possible that the Vryheid Front's program will not put it onto a more felicitous course. But the Vryheid Front may be able to convince a majority of South Africans that neo-apartheid (despite its historical associations), neo-liberalism, and confederalism can all coexist. Favoring the Vryheid Front is the South Africans' strong sense of irony.[9] These people might delight in the prospect of an Afrikaner volkstaat being obliged, as a purely practical matter, to serve black residents who would be powerfully represented to it. Similarly, South Africans, who appreciate irony, might come to understand how several volkstaats and a "core" South African state could, through their interaction, preclude the illiberalisms toward which the present liberal order is tending. Although the Vryheid Front faces a difficult challenge in making its case, its goal is neither hopeless nor unworthy.

---

[8] Authoritative projections of public expenditures are indicative. President Mandela's Minister without Portfolio, Jay Naidoo, responsible for the government's Reconstruction and Development Program, announced only weeks after the April, 1994 elections that the program's cost would be R80 billion to R90 billion, or more than double the figure estimated *before* the elections.

[9] My long residence in South Africa convinced me that their sense of irony is indeed widespread.

The Search for Reality: Trilling versus Parrington

James J. Novak

Let's face it—most educated Americans, except for their technical specialty at work, are literate only in the sense of being cinema literate. They do not read novels nor, for that matter, watch educational channels on television, but instead get their "literary" input from the talkies. At any dinner party, Hollywood chatter about Harrison Ford or Michelle Pfeiffer far exceeds references to John Updike, except, of course, around university crit-lit film departments. Woody Allen has replaced Hemingway, just as Sylvester Stallone has taken the part of Charles Lindberg. Indeed, when listening to the average Blockbuster-educated American, his confusion between the actor and the character played, and between the "truth" of the film and the reality of daily life, suggests that his divorce from reality is so complete that, were this the 1960s, we would consider his fractionated thought to be the result of constant and direct exposure to smoke from a joint.

More important, it is often disconcerting to discover that most Americans find one movie to be like another. There is no genre or, for that matter, any other film tradition. Viewers see what the filmmakers see, for they have entered into the Hollywood world, without even realizing their seduction. There has been a profound revolution in the American mind, not only from print to film but from one set of values to another through film. Few are aware how this change in cinema reality occurred, and how it was prepared by a similar change in the world of literature in the years before most Americans became cinema literate.

In his book, *Hollywood versus America,* Michael Medved noted that, starting in 1965 with *Easy Rider,* Hollywood movies underwent a major change, from portrayal of life in a positive and realistic sense to a more subjective, violent, and self-centered view of reality, not only regarding sex and religious values, but also in terms of an anarchic dislike of society, particularly their own. Medved's thesis was that from that time, movies left behind the middle classes, who less and less frequented serious movies, and increasingly appealed to the alienated or to those who share their views. This trend away from movies began long after the television became a national pastime and long before the video boom. Medved also maintains that Hollywood would earn more by returning to the ideas that permeated the film industry before 1965.[1]

---
[1] Michael Medved, *Hollywood versus America* (New York: Harper Collins, 1993).

What he did not do was investigate the origin of the ideas that shaped the modern cinema, the new world of violence, fantasy, and alienation.

The deeper question about the origin of this change emerged recently, when James Bowman, film critic for the *American Spectator,* spoke out. He addressed a fundamental issue that has been at the heart of literary and film criticism, at least since the 1940s but which has been obscured by the more easily understood issues of cinematic violence. Because the issue largely has been ignored, there has been a moral argument against film, one that, though valid, has proved sterile, primarily because the debate has ignored the more pressing, metaphysical problem of what Bowman calls "verisimilitude." By raising this issue he widened the debate, thereby reaching the deepest part of the discussion. He established a link to an old Lionel Trilling essay, "Reality in America." Before examining this link, let us review what Bowman wrote:

> This month I have examined a bunch of films from the end of summer kid flicks—including *Virtuosity, Hackers, Mortal Kombat, Lord of Illusions,* and *Desperado*—and have been confirmed in my belief that what is killing these movies is not the presence of filth, but the absence on the part of film makers and audience truth-to life—that is what we critics call "verisimilitude." Say what you like about sex 'n violence, they are part of the real world. But, increasingly, neither sex 'n violence nor anything else in the movies bears any resemblance to what we recognize from the real world. The movies have become a world of their own, and it is now all-but-universally considered enough that movies should represent to us a movie reality, which, in real world terms, is merely often fantastical.[2]

Bowman dates this change in the late 1970s, when *Star Wars* and *Indiana Jones* films were created by the mind of

> the unashamed movie fantasist who takes us by the arm and says, "Hey! You know that this stuff is fake anyway. You've seen all the old movies. All the plots, all the characters are familiar. There's nothing we can do (that has a hope of making money anyway) that will surprise you so what's the point in pretending, of going thought with the charade of suspense and character development and careful adumbration of the illusion that what you are seeing on the screen is real? It's better just frankly to acknowledge the truth: it's a movie, not real life, and therefore you've got to expect it to be fake."

Most upsetting about Bowman's review is not its truth, but the fact that the "audience" has bought into this so that film reality is no longer a reflection of "real" reality, but constitutes a universe of ideas and fantasies. While such movies are entertaining, they also are "childish" and "scary." It is a world of self-indulgence and an attack on society that bears no significant relation to "real" reality. Anyone who has heard foreigners overseas discuss American cinema and say that *Mississippi Burning* reflects "what America is really like," who believe that the school in the *Dead Poet's Society* is typical of American private schools, who believe that corruption of corporations and widespread racism are the norm, who have no sense of the fantasy in American films, finds such attitudes truly frightening. Most viewers are not as perceptive as Bowman.

By separating film reality from "real" reality, Bowman asked a far more fundamental question than the rest of his reviews would suggest. And while he did not condemn all films, he did open the discussion that follows, about the past.

---

[2] James Bowman, "The Talkies: Rotters," *The American Spectator* (October 1995): 68–69.

This debate over reality is what should be at the heart of literary and film criticism; for nearly fifty years it has not been. While it is impossible to determine when the issue first became important, one literary tempest in the 1940s may be cited as having been at the "crossroads where literature and politics meet." It occurred, Richard Hofstadter noted, when Lionel Trilling attacked the aesthetic principle of Vernon Parrington, once a leading critic of American literature, but now virtually forgotten. Hofstadter opened his essay on Parrington with a quotation from Trilling, then one of America's premier literary and social critics:

> The most striking thing about the reputation of V. L. Parrington, as we think of it today, is its abrupt decline. On the appearance in 1927 of the first two of his three volumes, the *Main Currents of American Thought* won more prompt and enthusiastic acceptance that the first important works of Turner and Beard. Liberal critics hailed it as a major work, and even old-fashioned guardians of American literature were cordial...[3]
>
> In a famous essay, "Reality in America," written in 1940, Lionel Trilling attributed to Parrington "an influence on the conception of American culture which is not equaled by that of any writer of the past two decades." Parrington's ideas, Trilling remarked, "are now the accepted ones, wherever the college course in American literature is given by a teacher who conceives himself to be opposed to the genteel and the academic and in alliance with the vigorous and the actual. And whenever the liberal historian of America finds occasion to take account of the national literature...[ellipses in Hofstadter] it is Parrington who is the standard and guide.... Parrington formulated in a classic way the suppositions about our culture, which are held by the American middle class, so far as that class is at all liberal in its social thought, and so far as it begins to understand that literature has anything to do with society."

Hofstadter continues:

> Even as late as 1950, when Parrington's reputation had gone far on its course of decline (hastened by Trilling's withering verdict that his mind was rather too predicable to be consistently interesting), Henry Steele Commager in *The American Mind* professed that his deepest intellectual debt was to Parrington.

Nevertheless, by 1940, according to Trilling, Parrington no longer was at the heart of the new literary scheme. Trilling criticized Parrington for having a deplorably typical American mind:

> Parrington does not often deal with abstract philosophical ideas, but whenever he approaches a work of art we are made aware of the metaphysics on which his esthetics is based. There exists, he believes, a thing called reality. It is one and immutable, it is wholly external, it is irreducible. Men's minds may waver, but reality is always reliable, always the same, always easily known. And the artist's relation to reality conceives to be a simple one. Reality being fixed and given, the artist has but to let it pass through him; he is the lens in the first diagram of an elementary book on optics; Fig. 1, Reality; Fig. 2, Artist; Fig. 1', Work of Art. Figs. 1 and 1' are normally in correspondence with each other. Sometimes the artist spoils this ideal relation by "turning away from" reality. This results in fantastic works, unreal and ultimately useless. It does not occur to

---

[3] Richard Hofstadter, *The Progressive Historians: Turner, Beard, and Parrington* (New York: Alfred A. Knopf, 1969), 349–50.
[4] Lionel Trilling, "Reality in America," in *The Liberal Imagination* (New York: Doubleday Anchor Books, Doubleday and Company, 1957), 2–3 (italics in original).

Parrington that there is any other relation possible between the artist and reality than this passage of reality through the transparent artist; he meets evidence of imagination and creativeness with a settled hostility, the expression of which suggests that he regards them as the enemy of democracy.[5]

This and this alone is the source of Trilling's condemnation of Parrington. He did have other criticisms, some quite good, others petty. But the issue of reality was the centerpiece. This is seen especially well when Trilling discuses Parrington's treatment of Hawthorne and Henry James on the one hand, and on the other, Theodore Dreiser. For Parrington, like other Progressives and populists of his era, praised Dreiser for his vigorous and realistic portrait of American life. In contrast, he found Hawthorne and James to be more introverted, more concerned with nuance, with the self, the irrational, with evil. Trilling calls the juxtaposition of James and Dreiser "the dark and bloody crossroads where literature and politics meet." This is a divide that still persists, despite the transition from literature to the cinema and from there through several changes, to Bowman and the summer flicks of 1995. Regardless of the validity of Parrington's judgment of Dreiser vis-à-vis Progressive politics, Parrington's insistence on realist portrayal should be the focus in considering contemporary films.

Let us now turn to a third source to see what Trilling meant by "the vigorous and the actual"—Alexander Bloom's *Prodigal Sons: The New York Intellectuals and Their World,* a book that celebrates the ascension of the Ellis Island New York intellectuals in American thought and letters. Bloom expanded on the debate between the two writers as follows:

> With the end of radical politics, the concept of radical criticism, which had developed in the 1930s, needed to be revamped to become suitable for the new liberal mentality. A liberal cultural position, however, already existed—one which grew out of the traditional liberalism and one which needed correction. For Trilling, this older view found its most influential exponent in Vernon Parrington, especially in his *Main Currents in American Thought.* This book had educated a generation, and it influence persisted despite travails of the past decade. Parrington's sensibility corresponded to the historical notions of progressivism, focusing on democracy as a "fighting faith." Trilling argued that Parrington took a single-minded approach to the literature and exhibited an always too predictable, rough hewn, social and economic determinism.
>
> Parrington's focus on the progress of history seemed too often to favor particular styles of writing. "Society is after all something that exists at the moment as well as in the future," Trilling noted. "And if one man wants to probe curiously into the hidden furtive recesses if the contemporary soul, a broad democracy and especially one devoted to reality should allow him to do so without despising him." Such a probing of the contemporary soul or the human unconscious was precisely the undertaking that Trilling thought essential...
>
> Trilling's explanation for Parrington's persistent importance highlights a basic division Trilling aimed to overcome. Parrington expressed the chronic American belief that there exists an opposition between reality and mind and that one must enlist oneself in the party of reality. This division mirrors Trilling's perception about the unnatural split between rational and emotional. He believed that revitalized liberalism required a literary and critical component. He also believed that the critic could best serve by delving

---

[5] Alexander Bloom, *Prodigal Sons: The New York Intellectuals and Their World* (New York: Oxford University Press, 1986), 194–95.

into the mind, the unconscious, the emotions. If a new liberal criticism was to emerge alongside the new liberalism, the perceived separation had to be overcome.

Trilling sought to demonstrate that the separation of "mind" and "reality" was inappropriate. He noted the differing attitudes that prevailed toward Theodore Drieser and Henry James. Dreiser had been "indulged" by liberal intellectuals, despite his literary inferiority, while James had seen accorded nothing but "liberal severity." A more appropriate sensibility would have understood Dreiser's weaknesses, but "our liberal, progressive culture tolerated Dreiser's vulgar materialism...feeling that perhaps it was not quite intellectually adequate but certainly very strong, certainly very real." James on the other hand, suffered because American instinctively believe that "an art which is marked by perception and knowledge...can never get through gross dangers and difficulties." The sad truth, Trilling concluded, is that in the American metaphysic, reality is always material reality, hard, resistant, unformed, impenetrable, and unpleasant. This attitude has led Americans to place the most trust in that mind "which most resembles this reality by most nearly reproducing the sensations it affords."

Parrington found fault with James for withdrawing from "the external world of action...to the inner world of questioning and probing," dealing "more and more with less and less"—in the end becoming "concerned only with the nuances." This is just where Trilling wants us to go, just what he wants us to be concerned with. This is the realm in literature that can now serve and which critics can describe.

And as Bloom says a few pages later:

Several years later, in a lecture on Freud, Trilling briefly returned to the question of the relation between the artist and his culture. "For literature, as for Freud, the test of culture is always the individual self." ...The function of literature, through all its mutations, has been to make us aware of the particularity of selves, and the high authority or the self in its quarrel with its society and its culture.... "Literature is in that sense subversive."

Thus Bloom takes us to the heart of the debate. It is not over Parrington's faults as a writer or over his choice of authors. It is over the very meaning of society and art. They do indeed joust at the dark and bloody crossroads.

Hofstadter summed this up and showed its effect by 1968:

The criticism that [Parrington] represented had always been under fire, and with the increasing academic influence of the New Criticism in the late 1930s and early 1940s literary interest turned from biographical, historical, sociological, and moral aspects of the literature and toward just those aspects that Parrington is least concerned with: toward a close and exclusively interior analysis of texts, toward a preoccupation with language and with mythological and symbolic aspects of writing, toward the literary manifestations of the unconscious and the irrational. By the early 1940s, a complete critical jargon had come into being, which sounded as though it had been contrived in a world wholly alien to that of Parrington and his generation; and by then, the very idea of any kind of literary history, as opposed to criticism, was decidedly on the defensive...

The mind of a man like Parrington was suspended, in honest doubt and hesitation, between the world of progressive agrarian or bourgeois and the world of the supposedly ascendant proletariat. The mind of the literary modernists is convinced beyond doubt or hesitation of the utter speciousness of bourgeois values, and is altogether without hope, without interest, in the proletariat. Moreover, aside from the effect of the New Criticism, readers were becoming interested in a kind of writing that made the pale modern-

---

[6] Bloom, *Prodigal Sons*, 197–98.

ism of Parrington's era seem to belong to the nineteenth century. The new post-war modernism, with its sensationalism, its extremes of love and violence, its affections for the picaresque and the anti-hero, its interest in madness as a clue to the human, its candor about sexuality and its belief that the modes of sexuality embody or conceal symbols that are universally applicable and revealing, its sense of outrage, its distrust of institutions, its profound destructive intention, its persistent and almost hypnotic fascination with the deepest abysses of the human personality, seemed in many ways to be a transvaluation of everything that Parrington cared about, and thrust writers of Parrington's type so sharply backward into the past that he now seemed (and with a certain truth) to have merged into the genteel tradition, to have become an old-fashioned moralist. Even the radical tendency of the new modernism had next to nothing in common with the radicalism of Parrington's time. Where a Parrington looked askance upon established institutions as the possible agents of human exploitation, judged issues from the standpoint of a certain sentimentality about the people, and questioned the inherited idea of progress only with sad regret, the radicalism of the new writing moved increasingly toward a ruthless individualism or a thoroughgoing anarchism, a complete indifference or hostility to the principles by which institutions are constituted, a mordant skepticism about progress and a disposition to see the mass of men with more revulsion than pity.[7]

While Trilling was not the only critic of his era responsible for increasingly subjective movies (he believed in any case that the novel, not the cinema, was the main medium of expression), this Trilling-Parrington spat is symptomatic of the mindset that has infested the cinematic world since *Easy Rider*. Hofstadter, writing in 1968, saw this world emerging from the anarchy and subversion that began undermining traditional values in the 1960s. And while the escape from reality certainly did not start in either Hollywood or literature in the 1960s, there is no doubt that by then it became critical.

This literary tempest teaches us that he who shows someone his metaphysics, also shows him his morals and his mind. Verisimilitude matters—perhaps Parrington deserves a new reading both in Hollywood and literary criticism.

---

[7] Hofstadter, *The Progressive Historians*, 355–56.

Good Death: Is Euthanasia the Answer?

Anthony M. Matteo

I cannot contemplate the issue of legalizing euthanasia without recalling my own father's struggle with lung cancer over twenty years ago. The malignancy was discovered in August of 1973. The disease was already so far advanced that surgery was ruled out. He was subjected to rounds of radiation and chemotherapy but to no avail. Fortunately, because his primary care physician did not favor futile medical measures, neither I nor other family members encountered resistance when we took my father from the hospital and brought him home. For the next nine months we witnessed the gradual and irreversible dissipation of his physical and mental capacities. Eventually, he lapsed into a coma, lingered in that state for about a week, and then mercifully passed away. Though we were greatly saddened by his death, we also felt deep relief that his and our ordeals were over. When the morticians came for his body, my father, who throughout his adult life had been a strapping individual of well over two hundred pounds, had been reduced by cancer to skeletal proportions.

Numerous sons, daughters, wives, and husbands, have kept similar vigils, struggling to cope as they beheld their parents or spouses dying in such a prolonged fashion. It is only natural, then, that the memory of that experience weighs heavily when they attempt to fashion a moral attitude toward euthanasia. I suspect, that, as in my own case, the experience inclines them in the direction of legalizing euthanasia. Moreover, even those persons who have not had such a first-hand encounter with "lingering death" no doubt recoil at the specter of their own or their loved ones' wishing for release from suffering as they languish in thrall to respirators and feeding tubes.

Such images becloud rational thinking about euthanasia and make its legalization, subject to appropriate safeguards, seem like a compassionate and progressive move that fosters both patient autonomy and the reduction of suffering. By linking such emotive images to the power of slogans such as "right to die" and "death with dignity," the proponents of legalizing euthanasia have, according to a number of polls, garnered majority support (over 60 percent) within the American public.[1]

---

[1] For a historical overview of polling data showing increasing public support for legalizing euthanasia, see Robert J. Blendon, Ulrike S. Szalay, Richard A. Knox, "Should Physicians Aid Their Patients in Dying?" *JAMA* 267 (20 May 1992), 2658–62; and Franklin G. Miller and John C. Fletcher, "Physician Assisted Suicide and Active Euthanasia," in *Physician-Assisted Death*, ed. J.H. Humber et al. (Totowa, N.J.: Humana Press, 1993) 76–79. On 8 November 1994 voters in Oregon narrowly approved a measure, subsequently declared unconstitutional by a U.S. district court, legalizing phy-

However, with just a bit of reflection, we can rather easily envision a number of possible negative long-term consequences of making "killing" a legitimate part of the medical armamentarium. Our initial emotional reactions must be tempered by the strictest rational scrutiny before we effect such a momentous change in traditional medical ethics.

I

Let us begin by noting that the contemporary moral controversy surrounds *active*, not *passive* euthanasia. Passive euthanasia—the refusal or withdrawal of extraordinary means of treatment such as life support systems for the terminally ill—enjoys almost universal acceptance among moral theorists. To sustain mere biological functions such as heart rate or respiration by artificial means when death is inevitable seems futile, wasteful, even arrogant to the vast majority of those who consider the matter dispassionately. Passive euthanasia is simply letting someone die naturally. It represents a rational acceptance of our fate as mortal creatures.

Nor does the current controversy center on measures that physicians might take to relieve discomfort in their patients and which might also "indirectly" hasten death. Increasing the dosage of, say, morphine to cope with escalating pain in a cancer patient might have the side effect of depressing the respiratory system and shortening that patient's life. However, the purpose of the physician's action in such a case is to alleviate the patient's pain, not directly to end his life. Few, if any, would question that the physician, faced with such medical circumstances, is acting morally if no other remedy for the pain is available.

But voluntary active euthanasia—taking direct steps with their consent to end the life of patients—is generating intense moral and political debate. Opponents of the practice cite what they consider a fundamental moral difference between passive and active euthanasia: whereas passive euthanasia is simply "letting someone die," active euthanasia is nothing less than killing another human being. Thus, they conclude that it is morally acceptable to remove life support systems from a terminal patient and let nature take its course, but morally unacceptable to meet his request for a quick and painless termination of his life to mitigate the travail of dying.

Proponents of legalized euthanasia question whether this neat distinction between "killing" and "letting die" is enough to win the day. It would seem that the situation is more complex than this simple moral dichotomy allows. Surely there are cases, such as self-defense, in which killing is justified; and certainly not all cases of letting someone die can be considered moral. If I see a child drowning in the local pool, for example, I ought to feel obligated to come to his assistance in some way, not simply stand by and let nature take its course. The point is that, by itself, the "killing"/"letting die" distinction is too unnuanced to be very helpful as a moral guide. To sort out such cases we need to attend not only to the act itself, but also to the *intention* of the actor.

Let's consider an analogy from the law. The legal differences between the varying degrees of murder and justifiable homicide do not turn solely on the act of killing itself. What is crucial for making the legal decision is determining the intention or motive of the accused. Was there premeditation? Was it an act committed in the heat

---

sician-assisted suicide for patients with less than six months to live. Physician-assisted suicide differs from euthanasia in that, instead of direct killing through, say, lethal injection, doctors supply patients with a lethal amount of drugs which the patients themselves injest.

of passion? Are there sufficient grounds to believe a claim that the accused was acting in reasonable self-defense? The culpability of the accused and what, if any, punishment to impose will depend on the answers to these questions, which speak directly to his mindset and motivation.

James Rachels applies a similar kind of analysis to voluntary active euthanasia and argues that its moral legitimacy cannot be assessed properly without taking into consideration motive or intention.

> Doctors are concerned only with cases in which the patient's life is of no further use to him, or in which the patient's life has become or will soon become a terrible burden.... The bare difference between killing and letting die does not, in itself, make a moral difference. If a doctor lets a patient die, for humane reasons, he is in the same moral position as if he had given the patient a lethal injection for humane reasons.[2]

Presumably when a physician follows the wishes of a terminal patient or his family and withdraws artificial means of life support (passive euthanasia), he does so because for this patient death has now become preferable to continued existence. Recognizing that the physician is motivated by mercy and compassion, we might find his action laudable. If, however, we could discern some sinister motivation behind this same deed (some deal, say, with family members to get their hands on their inheritance more quickly), we would quickly reverse this judgment.

Rachels contends that we ought to treat the case of active euthanasia in the same fashion. If a terminal patient facing slow degeneration requests a quick termination of his life, the motivation of the physician who honors this request may be identical to that of a colleague who practices passive euthanasia. A physician clearly may provide a patient requested lethal injection as an act of mercy and compassion. What counts here as far as moral appraisal is concerned is *not* merely the naked act of "killing" or "letting die" but also the intention that motivates either approach. For Rachels, then, voluntary active and passive forms of euthanasia, when performed for noble reasons, are at least morally equivalent. There may even be cases in which active euthanasia is morally superior because it involves less suffering for the patient.

Rachels' argument has a good deal of initial plausibility. It seems to capture what most people discern intuitively: if we assist a desperately ill person to end his life to stave off suffering when he would soon die anyway, we cause that person no harm. The power of this insight goes a long way toward explaining why prosecutors are loathe to indict and juries are loathe to convict in what they discern to be genuine cases of "mercy killing." Such cases seem to be instances of "noninjurious" killing. They differ from murder or manslaughter, or even infanticide or abortion, in that they do not deny patients valuable futures. As Don Marquis puts it:

> [T]he claim that the loss of one's future is the wrong-making feature of one's being killed does not entail...that active euthanasia is wrong. Persons who are severely and incurably ill, who face a future of pain and despair, and who wish to die will not have suffered a loss if they are killed.[3]

---

[2] James Rachels, "Active and Passive Euthanasia," *The New England Journal of Medicine* 292 (9 January 1975): 79.
[3] Don Marquis, "Why Abortion Is Immoral," *The Journal of Philosophy* 86 (April 1989): 191. Dan W. Brock develops a similar argument in "Voluntary Active Euthanasia," *Hastings Center Report* (March–April 1992): 14.

So it would seem that if we are to make a convincing case against voluntary active euthanasia, yet continue to countenance voluntary passive euthanasia, it will have to rest on grounds more compelling that the mere killing/letting die distinction.

At this juncture, one could make an appeal to the traditional religious objection to suicide: God is the author of life and to take one's life, or request that another assist one in so doing, is an affront to God's sovereignty over us. Thomas Aquinas provided a classic expression of this objection: "Life is God's gift to man, and is subject to His power.... Hence whoever takes his own life sins against God.... For it belongs to God alone to pronounce sentence of death and life."[4]

Of course, Aquinas wrote against the background of the Judeo-Christian concept of God as both the creator and providential sustainer of all his creatures. This concept instructs us to view all that befalls us as an integral part of God's eternal plan. We must, accordingly, endure our sufferings with the confidence that they contribute to some greater good, even if that is comprehended only by the divine mind. Such a moral view, then, requires that we steadfastly await the appointed hour when God will call us home. To hasten that time by taking our own life, with or without the assistance of another, implies a denial on our part of God's providential governance of his creation.

Those who possess such a faith in divine providence as a central motivational and inspirational factor in their lives are unlikely to request active euthanasia as a means to resolve the dilemma of lingering death. Their faith will serve as a bulwark against the sense of weariness, meaninglessness, and despair that might prompt others to choose death over continued existence.

But such a providential vision cannot be forcibly imposed on those who cannot bring themselves to embrace it. When not filtered through the prism of religious faith, human experience does not provide clear and incontrovertible evidence that the ultimate reality upon which the universe depends cares for human beings in a providential manner. In fact, on might argue that the lack of any evident proportion between the evil that human beings suffer and any recognizable greater good flowing therefrom indicates that, at best, the ultimate reality is indifferent to the plight of humanity. One who sees the world is such terms might find it ludicrous to assume that his premature exit from a condition of physical and emotional suffering could in any way affront the dignity of the mysterious power undergirding the entire universe. Hence, the rejection of active euthanasia on *purely* religious grounds would seem to be a matter of individual choice, not incumbent on all members of society regardless of their religious commitments.

A secular variant of the preceding religious argument against voluntary active euthanasia is that such a practice is "unnatural" because it runs counter to our primal instinct for survival. According to J. G. Williams,

> euthanasia does violence to this natural goal of survival. It is literally acting against nature because all the processes of nature are bent towards the end of bodily survival. Euthanasia defeats these subtle mechanisms in a way that, in a particular case, disease and injury might not.[5]

---

[4] Thomas Aquinas, *Summa Theologica* II, II, 64.
[5] J. G. Williams, "The Wrongfulness of Euthanasia," in *Social and Personal Ethics,* William H. Shaw, ed. (Belmont, Calif.: Wadsworth, 1993), 101–02.

The force of this argument rests on the assumption that acting in a way that is contrary to our survival instinct is *always* and *inalterably* wrong. But is our standard moral practice rooted in such an assumption? There are times when police, firefighters, and soldiers are called upon to control their fears and subordinate natural concerns about their own survival for the sake of the common good. If they loose their lives in the line of duty seeking to protect or rescue others, they are lionized as heroes, not castigated for having senselessly thrown their lives away. On the other hand, we consider it a great tragedy if a youth deeply depressed because of a failed relationship, or a middle-aged man distraught due to financial ruin, takes his own life in a moment of despair.

What underlies our different moral reactions to these cases? In the case of the valiant public servants we grant our moral approval because we recognize that they sacrificed their lives for some greater good. However, we react negatively to a suicide who has needlessly ended his life based on an emotionally distorted appraisal of his circumstances because no greater good was served by his self-destruction. Proper intervention could have shown him that there was a way out of his depression; that life was still worth living because numerous positive experiences were still possible.

It would seem that terminal patients, asked to justify their request for euthanasia, could argue that their moral status is more akin to that of valiant public servants than that of a suicide. If shortening their own period of suffering seems too self-serving a motivation, they could speak of their desire to relieve their families of emotional and financial burdens, or of their wish to see the use of the medical resources expended on their care directed to those who had a greater chance of a full future life. In other words, they could articulate at least a *prima facie* claim that their immediate, rather than protracted, demise would serve some higher purpose, and not be an act of heedlessly or selfishly throwing their lives away. In short, they could contend that, in their situations euthanasia represents a legitimate contravention of the self-preservative instinct in a direct moral line with other such contraventions that we already accept.

II

Although these represent plausible arguments in favor of voluntary active euthanasia, prudence dictates that we make a distinction between sufficient moral support for isolated, individual acts thereof and adequate moral grounds for "legalizing" the practice as a matter of legitimate and regular public policy. A complete moral analysis of the latter move requires a careful assessment of the possible long-term negative effects of legalization.

The easy availability of euthanasia might slowly but surely undermine our sense of moral obligation to care for the incurably and terminally ill. Rather than allow them to continue to sap our medical and emotional resources, we might begin to exert psychological pressure on them to do the "noble" thing by taking an early exit. Furthermore, there is the fear of the "slippery slope" effect, leading from voluntary to involuntary active euthanasia.

Caring for the sick can exact a heavy financial and emotional price on families and society. Where there is hope for recovery, such travail seems worth the cost. But, in the absence of such hope, what motivates medical personnel, family members, and society at large to bear such burdens? It is certainly not some strictly "utilitarian" consideration; indeed the "greatest good for the greatest number" might well be better served by a redirection or our wealth and efforts from the care of the terminally and incurably ill to some socially more useful purpose. The motivating force, then, would have to be some overriding sense of the "inherent" worth of individual persons that obligates us to care for them when they can no longer care for themselves. Therefore, one might contend that the general taboo against active euthanasia can be viewed as a way of safeguarding the inherent worth of the terminally and incurably ill when it is most in danger of being undermined by so called "practical" considerations.

Through the sole prism of cost/benefit analysis, one could quite easily come to see those in the final states of a fatal illness, or even those afflicted with slower degenerative maladies such as Alzheimer's or Lou Gehrig's disease, as better off dead than alive, not *primarily* for their own sakes, but for the sake of their families and society. If such analysis were to become prominent in our thinking, it would not be long until we reduced the terminally and incurably ill to *lebensunwertiges Leben* (life unworthy of life), that is, beings with the moral and legal status of expendable items whose continued existence is an unwarranted strain on our limited resources.

Proponents of legalized active euthanasia, however, believe that the practice can be kept voluntary and that abuses can be controlled. Safeguards such as mandatory euthanasia review committees, complete psychological evaluations, and the requirement of thorough documentation and reporting of euthanasia cases to relevant authorities could be put in place so that: (1) only those with terminal or incurable debilitating illnesses would be candidates for voluntary active euthanasia; (2) requests for euthanasia based on physical symptoms, such as chronic pain, would not automatically be honored; expert advice would have to be sought to discover whether the symptoms were treatable; (3) requests for euthanasia due to clinical depression (not uncommon among the terminally and incurably ill) would be detected and treated through therapeutic intervention; and (4) the only euthanasia requests that would be honored would be based on rational decisions made by competent patients, not the result of subtle or overt coercion by family or medical staff.[6]

With the protection afforded by such safeguards, proponents believe we can uphold the dignity and worth of individuals. Whether terminal and incurable patients desire a quick termination or wish to live their lives to their natural biological ends, their wishes will be respected. Thus, proponents contend, strictly utilitarian considerations will not prevail and we need not fear the emergence of some nightmare scenario in which the terminally or incurably ill are either systematically neglected or made of victims of involuntary euthanasia. Furthermore, since physician assisted suicide and voluntary active euthanasia currently occur *sub rosa,* abuses are probably already occurring which controlled legalization would curtail.[7]

If, on the one hand, the opponents of legalized euthanasia are right about the corrosive effects of lifting the moral and legal taboo against direct physicians' involve-

---

[6] For three proposals outlining detailed procedures aimed at preventing abuse of legalized voluntary active euthanasia and physician-assisted suicide see Margaret Battin, "Voluntary Euthanasia and the Risks of Abuse: Can We Learn Anything from the Netherlands?" *Law, Medicine and Health Care* 20 (Spring-Summer 1992): 133–43; Timothy E. Quill, Christine K. Cassel, Diane E. Meier, "Care Of The Hopelessly Ill: Proposed Clinical Criteria for Physician-Assisted Suicide," *The New England Journal Of Medicine* 327 (5 November 1992): 1380–83; and Franklin G. Miller, Timothy E. Quill, Howard Brody, John C. Fletcher, Lawrence O. Gostin, Diane E. Meier, "Regulating Physician-Assisted Death," *The New England Journal of Medicine* 331 (14 July 1994): 119–23.
[7] Margaret Battin, *Ethical Issues in Suicide* (Englewood Cliffs, N.J.: Prentice Hall, 1995), 215 and 224.

ment in the death of their patients, then the long term costs of legalization would outweigh the short term benefits it might bring in the way of reduced suffering and fulfilling the individual wishes of those incurable persons who desire an immediate termination of their lives. If, on the other hand, as the proponents of legalization contend, such fears are ill-founded if proper oversight is exercised, then one of the most powerful arguments against legalization is defeated. So we're left to ponder the decisive question: can this practice be effectively controlled?

III

With this question in mind, let us examine active euthanasia as practiced in the Netherlands. A series of court decisions, along with the concurrence of the Dutch Parliament and the support of the Royal Dutch Medical Society (KNMG), has made euthanasia and physician-assisted suicide *de facto* legal in that country. Dutch physicians can feel assured that if they follow guidelines purportedly guaranteeing: (1) the patient's decision for euthanasia is voluntary; (2) the patient is experiencing unbearable suffering that cannot be relieved by other means; (3) the attending physician consults with a colleague concerning the euthanasia decision; and (4) the local prosecutor is notified that death was caused by euthanasia, then no criminal charges will be brought against them.

To discover the actual extent of euthanasia in the Netherlands the government (in January, 1990) commissioned Professor Van Remmelink, attorney-general of the Dutch Supreme Court, to direct a study of euthanasia and other medical decisions concerning the end of life. The study consisted of detailed interviews with 405 physicians of varying specialties, a questionnaire sent to physicians of 7,000 deceased individuals, and a prospective survey in which physicians interviewed in part I provided details regarding every death in their respective practices for a period of six months after the initial interview. Physicians were granted anonymity and immunity from prosecution for all the information they revealed.

On the basis of its investigations the Remmelink report estimated that active euthanasia occurred in 1.8 percent (c. 2,300 cases annually) of all deaths in the Netherlands and physician-assisted suicide accounted for 0.3 percent (c. 400 cases annually) of total mortality. Of the participating physicians, 54 percent reported having performed active euthanasia or assisted suicide while granting only about one out of three requests for these practices. Furthermore, it was the doctor's primary or secondary intention to hasten death in 16,850 other cases by withholding treatment (8,750) or by prescribing opiates (8,100). Physicians recorded "death by euthanasia" on death certificates in only 454 cases. Thus, the vast majority of euthanasia deaths were certified by physicians as "death by natural causes." The Remmelink report also estimated that 0.8 percent of all deaths were due to active euthanasia without explicit request of the patient.[8]

The fact that the Remmelink report revealed cases of euthanasia without explicit request of the patient was disturbing in that such acts violated the "voluntariness"

---

[8] P. J. Van der Maas, Johannes J.M. Van Delden, Loes Pijnenborg, Caspar W.N. Looman, "Euthanasia and Other Medical Decisions Concerning The End Of Life," *Health Policy* 22 (September 1992): 193–94. An abbreviated version of this report appears in *The Lancet* 338 (14 September 1991): 669–74.

guideline and apparently confirmed the claims of critics about an inevitable slide from voluntary to involuntary euthanasia.[9] To allay such fears, the authors of the original report provided the following data in a subsequent publication:

> In 59% of LAWER [Life-terminating acts without explicit request] the physician had some information about the patient's wish; in 41% discussion on the decision would no longer have been possible.... The physician (specialist or general practitioner) knew the patient on average 2–4 years and 7–2 years, respectively. Life was shortened by between some hours and a week at most in 86%. In 83% the decision had been discussed with relatives and in 70% with a colleague. In nearly all cases, according to the physician, the patient was suffering unbearably, there was no chance of improvement and palliative possibilities were exhausted.[10]

One could, of course, raise questions about how accurate a portrait of euthanasia in the Netherlands the Remmelink report provides. It relies entirely on the responses of physicians uncorroborated by any other sources. In such a study it is vitally important to ask probing follow-up questions as a control technique to weigh properly the veracity of the respondents. This would seem especially important in cases of euthanasia without request of the patient where the tendency toward self-justification on the part of physicians is quite powerful. Yet, in an interview with the report's principal investigator, Dr. Paul Van der Maas, Dr. Herbert Hendin discovered that this technique was not generally employed. Hendin opines that, in the investigations that form the basis of the Remmelink report, maintaining a harmonious relationship with the respondents took precedence over sound social scientific procedure: "In the interests of maintaining that harmony, virtually all the explanations of the physicians in the study appear to have been accepted at face value even when follow-up questions seemed necessary."[11]

More troubling, however, when one reads between the lines of the Remmelink report, is the extent to which active euthanasia in the Netherlands has become, in essence, a private affair between patients, their families, and physicians with little in the way of regulatory rigor to ward off possible abuses. Based on his own study of euthanasia in the Netherlands, Dr. Carlos Gomez concludes:

> Neither the courts nor the other branches of the Dutch government seem to play as active a role in managing and restricting euthanasia as the guidelines would imply, nor as defenders of the practice in the Netherlands have suggested. The role of both participant and regulator has fallen to the medical practitioners, with what seems to be the tacit consent of most of the rest of Dutch society.[12]

This seems to undercut the argument, at least as far as the Dutch experience is concerned, that *de facto* or *de jure* legalization of euthanasia will bring the practice

---

[9] Richard Fenigsen, "A Case Against Dutch Euthanasia," *Hastings Center Report* 19 (January-February 1989): 25.
[10] Loes Pijnenborg, Paul J. Van Der Maas, Johannes J. M. Van Delden, Caspar W. N. Looman, "Life-Terminating Acts without Explicit Request of Patient," *The Lancet* 341 (8 May 1993): 1196.
[11] Herbert Hendin, "Seduced by Death: Doctors, Patients, and the Dutch Cure," *Issues in Law & Medicine* 10 (1994): 156.
[12] Carlos Gomez, *Regulating Death: Euthanasia and the Case of the Netherlands* (New York: Free Press, 1991), 124.

"above ground" and foster effective oversight to prevent abuse. In language even more forceful than that of Gomez, John Keown proclaims:

> [A]s the evidence marshalled by Gomez and others clearly indicates, all that is known with certainty is that euthanasia in the Netherlands is being practiced on a scale vastly exceeding the "known" (truthfully reported and recorded) cases. There is little sense in which it can be said, in any of its forms, to be under control. As even a supporter of legalized euthanasia such as Professor Leenen has observed, not only is there an "almost total lack of control on the administration of euthanasia," but the "present legal situation makes any adequate control of the practice of euthanasia virtually impossible."[13]

Few proponents of legalized euthanasia in America favor the implementation of the Dutch model in our nation. Given our greater size, diversity, economic and social divisions, plus our uneven and sometimes impersonal distribution of health care, they recognize the increased likelihood of abuse occurring in our midst.[14] Nonetheless, they have faith that some mix of regulatory measures will provide sufficient public scrutiny to control the process. Of course, whether or not such measures would succeed, is a speculative question to which no empirical answer can be given in advance. However, there is good reason to believe that attempts to regulate a regime of legalized active euthanasia would represent a chimerical quest.

Since active euthanasia is such a "camouflageable" deed, there would seem to be a catch 22 inherent in the effort to regulate it. To the extent that there is strict oversight to prevent abuses, involving genuine threats of professional sanctions and legal prosecution, doctors will be disinclined to report truthfully about cases of euthanasia. To the extent that doctors are granted *de facto* immunity from such threats, more cases will be reported but with little actual control over abuses. Given the already overburdened status of the American medical and legal systems, the latter scenario (*de facto* immunity with little actual control) would be more likely to occur.

Furthermore, the primary justification put forth to legalize active euthanasia, that is, the alleviation of unbearable suffering, requires physicians to make highly subjective judgments. As Robert Barry points out,

> suicide to abolish suffering and pain is uncontrollable in principle because there are no objective criteria to identify those forms of suffering that warrant self-execution and those that do not. "Analgesic" or "therapeutic" suicide cannot be controlled because there are no clear and evident differences between the various kinds of mental and physical suffering that would enable law and morality to differentiate those that should justify self-execution from those that should not.[15]

Is a cancer patient with a prognosis of six months to live a proper candidate for euthanasia while another, with a life expectancy of one year, is not? Will a euthanasia committee accede to the wishes of a patient for an early exit when pain is only 70 percent controlled but deny the same release to one whose pain is 85 percent controlled? Will those suffering from Lou Gehrig's disease be approved for euthanasia

---

[13] John Keown, "On Regulating Death," *Hastings Center Report* (March-April 1992): 42.
[14] Miller, "Regulating Physician-Assisted Suicide," 120; and Battin, "Voluntary Euthanasia and the Risks of Abuse: Can We Learn Anything from the Netherlands?" 138.
[15] Robert Barry, *Breaking the Thread of Life* (New Brunswick, N.J.: Transaction Publishers, 1994), 277.

but those with Alzheimer's be rejected? Can any euthanasia committee, no matter how well-meaning, ever judge objectively and in a principled fashion when attempting to disentangle the physiological from the psychological components of the patient's suffering in the many requests it is likely to review? And, even allowing that the Dutch physicians interviewed by the Remmlink commission alleged denying two out of three euthanasia requests, would we Americans, given our near obsession with "individual rights," stand for such medical paternalism if active euthanasia were legal? Such considerations lend great weight to Barry's conclusion that

> it is not just that there are no clear differences between different kinds of suffering, but it is also not clear what level of suffering is sufficient to justify self-killing. Ultimately, determining these would have to be left to the individual, for neither law nor society could judge according to an objective standard when suffering became intolerable, and this would make it impossible to impose any sort of meaningful controls on it.[16]

Finally, it would be difficult, if not impossible, to devise procedures to guarantee the genuine "voluntariness" of euthanasia requests by patients. Overt coercion is not likely to be the culprit here. Instead, the threat would come from social pressures on dying patients, especially those requiring extensive care, to behave "nobly"—that is, in consideration of their survivors' finances and emotions—by requesting euthanasia. According to Richard Fenigsen, just such pressures have already taken hold in the Netherlands.

> For twenty years the population of Holland had been subjected to all-intrusive propaganda in favor of death. The highest terms of praise have been applied to the request to die: this act is "brave," "wise," and "progressive." All efforts are made to convince people that this is what they ought to do, what society expects of them, what is best for themselves and their families.[17]

In sum, it is not alarmist fantasy to fear the harm that legalizing euthanasia might wreak upon our sense of duty to care for the most vulnerable in our midst. Rather, there are good grounds to believe that, like opening Pandora's mythical box, such a fundamental alteration in our medical and legal tradition would lead to the release of new social ills that would defy even our most well intentioned efforts at effective regulation and control.

IV

Given the societal dangers posed by the legalization of active euthanasia, it would seem to make more moral sense, and be a more prudent manifestation of compassion, to find some alternative way to meet the physical, psychological, and spiritual needs of the terminally and incurably ill. In fact, such an alternative already exists in the form of home and institutional hospice care.

Central to the hospice approach is the acceptance of death as the "natural" terminus of our lives. This approach opposes the continuation of highly invasive medical

---

[16] Barry, *Breaking the Thread of Life,* 278. In this context, should any legally recognized right to die extend to persons having serious mental illnesses?

[17] Fenigsen, "A Case Against Dutch Euthanasia," 24.

procedures after it is clear that they no longer have a curative effect. Instead, hospice treatment focuses its efforts on "palliative" care to control pain effectively and provide needed psychological and spiritual support to patients and their families. Hospice care takes its orientation from the proposition that pain and despair lead patients to request an early exit from life. Accordingly, the relief of such pain and despair by the compassionate intervention of dedicated professionals is a far more life-affirming approach than acceding to the pleas of desperately ill individuals to have their lives terminated. From the hospice perspective, true concern for the incurably sick and dying, as well as for the maintenance of the integrity of the healing professions, would be far better served by a proliferation of hospices as opposed to broad based legalization of active euthanasia. In the words of Dr. David Cundiff:

> We have the knowledge and the means to assure that no terminally ill person need beg for death to end his or her suffering. We need the resolve to spread this precious knowledge. Universally available, excellent quality hospice medicine is the life-affirming alternative to the hopelessness of euthanasia.[18]

Proponents of legalized euthanasia do not gainsay the important contributions of the hospice movement toward improving care for the dying. However, they resist the claim that the availability of hospice care ought to rule out the possibility of legal active euthanasia. As Derek Humphry puts it:

> Euthanasia supporters argue that both options are important for a terminally ill adult. While almost all euthanasists would probably resist the idea of dying in a hospice, none would seek to prevent this style of palliative care for others.[19]

Undergirding this argument is the assumption that people are autonomous individuals possessing a broad right to privacy, including a "right to die." From this perspective those who wish the assistance of medical professionals in ending their lives ought not to be forbidden by the state from having their wishes honored. According to Ronald Dworkin, the decision either to see the dying process to its normal biological end or to request its early termination by active euthanasia turns on such highly personal ethical or religious convictions that the state should not intervene and impose its will. He dramatically proclaims: "Making someone die in a way that others approve, but he believes a horrifying contradiction of his life, is a devastating, odious form of tyranny."[20]

What are we to make of this purported "right to die"? Certainly we should not view it as some unencumbered right to self-destruction. We would not stand idly by and watch another kill himself, let alone assist him in the process, simply because he had announced that his life was no longer worth living. We know that the vast majority of suicide attempts are carried out by people beset with diagnosable and treatable psychiatric disorders.[21] As a result, we would not dream of arguing that suicide hotlines or crisis intervention teams, which seek to help such troubled souls and dissuade them

---

[18] David Cundiff, *Euthanasia Is Not The Answer* (Totowa, N.J.: Humana Press, 1992), 162.
[19] Derek Humphry, *The Right To Die* (New York: Harper & Row, 1986), 181.
[20] Ronald Dworkin, *Life's Dominion* (New York: Alfred A. Knopf, 1993), 217.
[21] Herbert Hendin and Gerald Klerman, "Physician-Assisted Suicide: The Dangers of Legalization," *American Journal of Psychiatry*, 150 (January 1993): 143.

from self-destruction, are violating some fundamental right to end one's life whenever one sees fit. Experience teaches us that suicide attempts are generally acts of desperation that appear irrational to objective observers precisely because other nondestructive remedies to the dilemmas at issue are available. Surely, then, only a cruel and craven society would countenance, let alone actively support, irrational self-destruction in the name of unfettered self-determination by proclaiming a generalized "right to die."

But what of the terminally and incurably ill? Are the remedies available to them so few, their futures so limited, that the desire for immediate death represents a rational choice that a good society ought to respect? Does it make sense, then, to talk of a "right to die" in their restricted circumstances?

It should be noted that those requesting active euthanasia are not, as proponents of legalization would have us believe, psychologically distinct from others who contemplate self-destruction.

> [L]ike other suicidal individuals, patients who desire an early death during a terminal illness are usually suffering from a treatable mental illness, most commonly a depressive condition. Strikingly, the overwhelming majority of the terminally ill fight for life to the end. Some may voice suicidal thoughts in response to transient depression or severe pain, but these patients usually respond well to treatment for depressive illness and pain medication and are grateful to be alive.[22]

Clearly what such patients need and deserve is not confirmation of their suicidal intent but compassionate professional intervention so that they may experience minimal pain and adequate psychological and spiritual support. But what if, after such intervention, there are still some patients who request euthanasia, asserting a fundamental right to structure the final chapter of their lives as *they* see fit? Such patients would presumably find enduring their disease to the end a humiliating experience that they would rather not undergo. They would feel that denying them the option of seeking assistance for an early exit would be an affront to their dignity.

Indeed, many who view their lives in this fashion will choose to end them by their own hands early in the progression of their dying. But if not, the hard truth is that such individuals do not live in a social vacuum: what they subjectively perceive as "good" for themselves may not be "good" for society in general. We would run great risks if, even out of a sense of compassion, we were to enmesh the medical profession in a regime of active euthanasia to comply with the wishes of such patients. They can make a moral claim upon us for care and solicitude, not for complicity in their self-destruction. Prudence dictates that we reject a "right to die" construed in the fashion of advocates like Dworkin and Humphry; the stakes involved are simply too high.

The marvels of modern medicine will make it possible for most of us who inhabit places like North America or Western Europe to enjoy longer lives on average than our ancestors. We shall not be felled at relatively young ages by traditional infectious killers such as smallpox, cholera, or tuberculosis. The downside of this greater longevity is that many of us will experience a "lingering death" caused by cancer or some other degenerative disease. Hence, we face the potent medical and moral challenge of how to deal with this pattern of dying. Legalizing active euthanasia and physician-assisted suicide is one suggested response. Despite the theoretical argu-

---

[22] Hendin and Klerman, "Physician-Assisted Suicide: The Dangers of Legalization," 143.

ments in its favor, I have tried to show that, due to its most likely consequences, it is a response we ought to reject. A far less socially perilous and far more life-affirming option would be to alter our medical practice to make available widespread palliative care in lieu of continued curative and life-support measures when the latter have become futile. By extending the hospice approach to all who need it we can best exercise the concern and compassion that morality demands without running the sizable risk of undercutting any further the fragile sense of human life's inherent worth and dignity.

The Prophet Armed

Jeremy Pizzola

John L. Esposito: **Islam and Politics.** Syracuse, N.Y.: Syracuse University Press, 1991. Third edition, 344 pp. $16.95.

In his third edition of *Islam and Politics,* John Esposito brings the reader a concise overview of the origins of Islam and its close, often turbulent relation to politics in the Middle East. His use of profiles of past and present Islamic leaders combines well with the often dry explanations of the modernist-revivalist controversies that continue to be a source of conflict in today's Islamic world. With this as his background, Esposito puts forth a compelling assessment of the issues that Islam faces in dealing with the twin demands of the Islamic faith and the immediate pressure of today's political atmosphere.

The book develops a foundation for understanding Islamic culture by explaining the origins of the faith and the start of the Islamic empire from the renaming of the city Yathrib to Medina under Muhammad's rule in 622 A.D., though the end of the Abbasid caliphate in 1258 A.D. From the very start Esposito explains that Islam was a sociopolitical as well as religious movement, and the despite the efforts of the colonial powers as well as the more recent modernizing forces in the region, Islam has remained one of the most critical factors in the organization and rule of the Middle East. Esposito also takes this time to explain the three phases of the caliphate (Rightly Guided Caliphs, Umayyad dynasty, and the Abassid caliphate) and how the fights over succession led to major divisions within the Islamic community that continue to be points of contention. He does an excellent job of making the reader aware that many of the conflicts within the Islamic world go back hundreds of years, and he provides the feeling of continuity necessary to begin to understanding the workings of the delicate balance of power in the region.

The basic foundation of all rule for the followers of Islam is derived from the Quran, and the mandate "Obey God and the Prophet" (3:32). It was in this way that Muhammad's rule was legitimized, and more importantly the leaders who followed (caliphs), though not prophets, were the legitimate heirs to this position and legitimized rulers and leaders of the Islamic community charged with upholding Islam and spreading the rule and the will of God. Given this view, the separation of religion and state even in modern Middle Eastern nations is as unthinkable to a Moslem as creating a Federal Church of Christ would be to most Americans. Esposito makes it clear that legitimate rule in these nations is derived from religious beliefs. Those without the legitimacy granted by religion must maintain their rule by force, and even in the most extreme circumstances, such as Turkey under the rule of Mustafa Kemal in the early 1920s, the secularization of the state could not be completed. He places the governments in the region into one of three general and readily understandable categories: secular, Islamic, and Muslim. In Turkey a totally secular path was chosen under Kemal, and the Turkish government, stressed nationalism and ethnicity to legitimatize its rule.

The long process of removing Islam from the workings of the Turkish government included abolishing the Sultanate in 1922 and the Caliphate in 1924. In 1926 the Islamic-based civil code was replaced by an Italian-Swiss-based code, and Kemal began what is widely accepted today as a dismantling of any possible alternative to his leadership, which for the most part happened to be the Islamic orders and organizations of Turkey. After World War II these efforts to expunge Islam from the workings of the state were slowly reversed; public education began to teach mandated religion courses in 1950, unless the parents specifically objected. The reemergence of Islamic political groups and their quickly growing power led to a reactionary military junta seizing power in 1980 and cracking down on those groups that would see the secularization of Turkey reversed. Nevertheless, 99 percent of the Turkish population remains Muslim, and Islam provides the basis for the opposition groups now contending with Turkish proponents of secularization.

Esposito uses animated historical narrative as well as dispassionate analysis to explain the Islamic orientation of states such as Saudi Arabia, which proclaim Islamic law and use it to legitimize their rule and to better their positions in dealing with other Muslim countries. Strife continues to exist within Islamic rule and comes from sectarians who resent the rule of the Saud clan, or from Shii Muslims who have been at odds with Sunni Muslims over the true approach to Islam since the assassination of the fourth Caliph, Ali, in 661 A.D.

The third group of governments in the Muslim world try to synthesize a modernist and Western approach to social and political rule with the Islamic heritage. This group is typefied by Iran, which identifies itself as Muslim but has a non-Islamic history as well. After World War II Reza Khan tried to appeal to Zoarastrianism as a state religion to compete with Islam. The pendulum swung back with the ascension to power of Khomeini, as Iran moved toward becoming an Islamic state. But events before and after his death only confirmed that Iran was a state with both Western and Islamic traditions. Its government tends naturally toward being a Muslim state with a heavy non-Islamic component.

The question of how to reconcile the traditional Islamic past with Western pressures to secularize as well as the natural contention between separate cultures within the Muslim world have led some to call Islam a dying force, incompatible with modernity and the demands of a modern society. Esposito's book disputes this position by pointing to the reemergence of Islam as a political power in such countries as Iran, and by stressing the inability of Turkey and, to a lesser extent, Libya to completely secularize their governments. Esposito takes the time to explain the parallel development of Christianity throughout the Roman Empire and its changing relation to modern society. From its inception, Esposito explains, Islam has been by its nature openly political. There is no possible separation of church and state for the true follower of Islam. Under the Caliphs there was a fusion of powers, and slowly there came to be a two-swords approach with regards to church/state relations through most of the Muslim world. At the same time, a tendency has been at work to fuse the powers of church and state as Islamic factions bring to bear their influence in today's world.

John Esposito's third edition of *Islam and Politics* is an engaging book that clearly addresses many issues facing Muslim societies, while providing enough history to clarify contemporary upheavals. We in the West often take for granted the process of secularization and we underestimate the importance if not primacy of religion in the affairs of Muslim nations. Esposito's book will serve to cure the reader of that shortsighted view.

Globalizing Politics

Paul Gottfried

Shadia B. Drury: **Alexandre Kojève: The Roots of Postmodern Politics.**
New York: St. Martin's Press, 1994. 274 pp. $19.95.

In her latest book Shadia Drury takes up a discussion she had begun in her first work, on the political theorist and classical scholar Leo Strauss and his disciples. According to Drury, Strauss and those who studied with him at the University of Chicago nurtured ulterior motives in the way they interpreted political texts. Distinguishing between the exoteric and esoteric readings, Straussians have claimed to hold the true key to understanding long-dead authors. This understanding, for them, is based on the fact that political theorists in the past could not always express themselves openly. Because of governmental and ecclesiastical pressures and their concern about saying more than was proper for intellectually immature readers, thinkers through the ages, according to Straussians, have hidden their thoughts behind public professions of orthodox religious and philosophical views. The Straussians claim to be able to decode this style of writing and to locate the skeptical core in the speculations of those they study.

Drury maintains that such claims highlight a basic contradiction characteristic of the Straussian involvement in education and politics. Though the students of Strauss typically express a belief in global democracy and in America's mission to spread political equality, they are clearly of two minds about democratic rule. Drury believes their true teacher more that Strauss was Friedrich Nietzsche, who combined nihilism with a belief in creative elites. While Strauss and his students have warned against the nihilistic and antidemocratic aspects of Nietzsche's work as a cultural and social critic, they have also absorbed what they condemn. They present themselves as a natural aristocracy who are indispensable as political teachers in a society without a hereditary noble class.

In the 1980s many Straussians rose to high place in the Reagan administration, particularly in foreign affairs and in agencies such as the NEH, USIA, and Department of Education. Straussians have also developed a reputation for academic politics and gained considerable power for themselves and their allies in political science departments at the Universities of Chicago and Toronto, Claremont College, and other major centers of higher learning. Members of this school of thought have also acquired notoriety for their clannishness and bellicosity. They are thought to hold the same predictable views on a wide range of subjects and to distinguish themselves from others in terms of their adherence to certain cultic opinions.

A major problem with Drury's critique is the forced attempt to depict Straussianism as an antidemocratic threat from the right. Having worked in the same subject, it seems to me that Drury may exaggerate the rightist tendencies in the Straussian legacy. The overshadowing intellectual and political threat for Strauss, a Jewish refugee from Nazi Germany, was what he and his disciples called "historicism," the beliefs that the Good is derivative from the historical tradition, and that one cannot properly discuss virtue and justice outside of particular historical circumstances. Straussians view "antirationalism" as embodied in the appeal to History as a source of and justification for moral action. They attribute this antirationalism to Nazism, postmodernism, and, more generally, to the "wave of modernity" that has produced the antiliberal movements of the twentieth century. Strauss sketches their picture of erupting irrationalism and the war against liberalism in *Natural Right and History* (1951); and whatever other agendas one may ascribe to him and his followers, they are certainly explicit about their rationalist political values. Strauss specifically singles out for considerations the historicist enemies of the Enlightenment, starting with Edmund Burke, who tried to equate the Good with the traditional. Such thinkers are accused of repudiating reason as a basis of political theory and political practice. And Strauss and his disciples have expressed their belief in the need to construct regimes on the basis of plans devised by individual minds. If they seem in this regard elitist, there is still no reason to assume her a Nietzschean subtext. The philosophers in the eighteenth-century France and the Bolsheveiks in twentieth-century Russia likewise combined rationalist projects with elitist operational modes.

In her newest book Drury offers fresh interpretive insight about her subjects. She points to a plausible genealogy for the evolution of the Straussian thinking—and derivatively of the political currents to which it has contributed. She looks at the life and thought of Alexandre Kojève (1902–1968), a Russian émigré who settled in Paris and taught for many years at the College de France. A contributor to the Hegelian left, Kojève read into the dialectic philosophy constructed by Hegel Marxist themes which he claimed to have found first in Hegel. Drawing selectively from Hegel's discussion of the master-slave relationship in *The Phenomenology of the Spirit* (1807), Kojève articulated a supposedly Hegelian vision of the down trodden coming to power and thereafter creating a world-state. This state, Kojève hoped, would transcend the limits of nationality and inherited cultural-political distinctions. Kojève identified Marxist-Hegelianism with the triumph of universality; and as a minor official of the European Common Market who praised Stalinist Russia he sought to promote his "inevitable" dream if a globalist end of history.

For Kojève, the two roles, working for the common market and apologizing for Staling, were not mutually contradictory. Both led beyond nationalism, albeit in one case through tyranny and in the other through supranational administration. As Kojève confessed in an exchange with Strauss on Xenopons dialogue "Hiero," tyranny is an acceptable price for the establishment of a world state. Though Xenophon's Syracusan tyrant is a ludricous sensualist, Kojève seizes on this partly satirical text to make a plea for cosmic despotism. World unity and rational order, however defined, seemed the goals for which Kojeve would gladly sacrifice the rights of others to life and liberty. He also saw these goals as being foreshadowed in Hegel's *Phenomenology,* various revolutionary governments, and Eurobureacracy.

Though Strauss raises objections to Kojève's vision, his own disciples have entertained fewer reservations about its author. Complimentary references to Kojève abound in their work, and Kojève's interpretations of Hegel cast a particularly strong spell on the late Allan Bloom, who quotes one as an authority on the other. Most significantly, "The End of History" argument advanced in 1991 by Francis Fukuyama, a student of Bloom's, illustrates the distinctively Kojevian reading of Hegel.

Fukuyama's prophecy of democratic capitalism becoming a universal political-economic norm and driving conflict from the historic stage reprises the Kojevian theme of a bureaucratic socialist end of History. Note that Kojève accepted the possibility of more than one kind of universal order. Fukuyama's global democratic order can be seen as convey the same hope for an homogenized humanity as the one expressed by Kojeve.

Drury understands and documents this Straussian-Kojevian connection. She also makes clear that Straussian hermeneutics and Kojevian Hegelianism are both concerned with the exercise of power—and not merely with speculative questions. What she does not fully explain is why the globalist vision basic to both is specifically "postmodern." While postmodernists seem interested in discrediting universalist assumptions about knowledge and morality, Drury's subjects are concerned about imposing a vision of global order, disguised as a political inevitability. While postmodernists, moreover, proclaim the value of particularity, Kojève and the Straussians try to fit politics and culture into a rationalist scheme. Drury may have no use for either Straussians or postmodernist, but what she does not demonstrate to this critic's satisfaction is that they overlap.

A Diseased Democracy

Melanie Burke Reiser

Christopher Lasch: **The Revolt of the Elites and the Betrayal of Democracy.**
New York: W. W. Norton & Company, 1995. 276 pp. $22.00.

As a new century rapidly approaches, scholars are reflecting on the current state of democracy in the United States and whether or not the democratic tradition will fare well in the future. With the crime rates soaring, an increasingly apathetic public, the supremacy of television as a source of information and as a childcare provider, and a pervasive concept of individualism, it is apparent that the United States is in the midst of vast turmoil and that democracy may not be the solution to our political problems. Christopher Lasch's final work, *The Revolt of the Elites and the Betrayal of Democracy,* is a powerful and diagnostic analysis of the current ailments of American democracy. Lasch's work offers a historical perspective, expansive enough to be incorporated into modern American history courses, on the rise of a new ruling class and how this class is posing a threat to the traditional definitions of democracy.

The Revolt of the Elites and the Betrayal of Democracy begins with Lasch's definition of the "elites" in a section entitled "The Intensification of Social Divisions." Lasch contends that the new elites in both American and international life are the people who control the flow of information and money and who dictate the trends in public debate. Lasch traces the emergence of these elites to the Progressive era, as the idea of participatory democracy was replaced by a technological mode of government in which it was believed that the masses would be better served, due to their inherent ineptness, by having their actions dictated by "experts." With an increased division among the classes, these experts have extended their realm to encompass the media and to preside over higher education. These elites, by Lasch's interpretation, have managed to redefine success as upward mobility. People are no longer interested in practicing self-government and are now virtually obsessed with a "quick-fix" mentality where anything and everything is done so that one can rapidly ascend into the upper echelons of society.

After having given a clear and convincing argument about America's dominance by an elite class, Lasch devotes the remainder of his work to buttressing two propositions: (1) democracy essentially implies an acceptance of common standards which America is clearly lacking at present; and (2) the recent relegation of political debate to elites obsessed with rhetoric allows a minority to control discussion in direct defiance of the democratic tradition of public debate.

Lasch states that "common standards are absolutely indispensable to a democratic society. Societies organized around a hierarchy of privilege can afford multiple standards, but a democracy cannot. Double standards mean second-class citizenship" (88). He convincingly argues that double standards do in fact prevail in our supposedly democratic society, and he seems particularly disturbed by the closing off of debate about affirmative action. In his call for explicit democratic consensus Lasch seems to be echoing Jean-Jacques Rousseau who insisted on the need for civil religion. Lasch calls for a better clarified democratic dogma when he states, "Even if we can't agree in the definition of a good life—and it could be argued that we have not yet seriously made the effort—we can surely agree on minimal standards of workmanship, literacy, and general competence. Without these, we have no basis on which either to demand respect or grant it" (88). It is America's misguided belief that tolerance in all aspects of life is the foundation of American democracy which leads to the acceptance of second-rate workmanship and can ultimately lead to the demise of any semblance of self-rule, says Lasch.

Although his points are well presented, Lasch also betrays a defect that is all too common in our time. *The Revolt of the Elites and the Betrayal of Democracy* is yet another diagnostic work without any proposed cure. He offers an accurate portrayal of the current state of American democracy, but that is all the reader gets. Lasch calls for an establishment of certain standards, but fails to outline what these standards should be. He uses the studies of Amitai Etzioni to show that while the nation appears to be brutally divided among liberal and conservative ideologies, we are in fact in accord over certain basic standards. However, he feels that problems arise when we try to apply these standards to certain policy issues and concludes by painting a bleak picture about the possibility of reaching a set list of democratic standards by saying that such a development would drastically alter the overburdened market and the political party system. Such a reconstruction of the American system is virtually inconceivable, he argues. In the end, Lasch may resemble someone caught in a maze: every time he looks for an escape, he runs head-on into a wall.

But the second contention about the "decline of civil discourse" merits attention. Lasch states, "It is the act of articulation and defending our views that lifts them out of the category of 'opinions,' gives them shape and definition, and makes it possible for others to recognize them as a description of their own experience as well. In short, we come to know our own minds only by explaining ourselves to others" (170). Yet the public has ceased to explain themselves. Instead the elite debate among themselves, and a disillusioned America becomes mindlessly polarized along party lines after hearing politicians circumvent the issues by means of catch phrases and media-approved jargon.

In showing how the tragic decline in debate has created an apathetic nation run by the few, Lasch undertakes a thorough historical investigation. He shows that the media once took identifiable stances on issues and created controversy and debate. However, the media has refused to be honest about its own activity and now pretends to present the facts and refrain form debate. The American public listens to misrepresented opinions and confuses them with "facts." Lasch also traces the history of public education and shows that contrary to the vision of educator Horace Mann, today's schools avoid controversy at all costs. The result is an "educated" group which often cannot write, let alone express their beliefs in intellectual discourse.

Yet, the most interesting argument that Lasch makes in regard to the loss of debate is that the decline of the neighborhood may be contributing to this result. He states that "the decline of participatory democracy may be directly related to the disappearance of third places. As neighborhood hangouts give way to suburban shopping malls, or, on the other hand, to private cocktail parties, the essentially political art of conversation is replaced by shoptalk or personal gossip. Increasingly conversation literally has no place in American society. In its absence, how, or better, where can political habits be acquired and polished?" (123). Americans have lost their ability to debate, and this has left the door open for elites to prescribe what Americans should think.

Throughout his book Lasch is trying to determine the role of democracy in an elitist society. He states that we need to look beyond the question of whether democracy can survive and ask if democracy deserves to survive. Yet, with all the evidence that Lasch provides for a lack of public debate, the decline in public life, the controlling hand of elites, and a failure to have an established list of standards, it seems that what he should be asking is whether democracy currently exists. Lasch fails to entertain that question, but speaks instead of a redefinition and reinvention of democracy. Never in his book does Lasch define his idea of democracy, so that he wanders from definition to definition without discussing whether or not America is now an aristocracy of information bearers.

The final section of Lasch's work, "The Dark Night of the Soul," stands apart from the rest of the book. Here Lasch attempts to trace the religious foundation of democracy by describing how the therapeutic state replaced the religious one. He argues that America abandoned her religious roots, or reformed them beyond recognition, to suit an individualistic mentality. Meanwhile Americans have embraced the notion of Science as savior. Lasch concludes his work by speculating about whether religion will restore democracy. This too demonstrates Lasch's failure to come up with probable cures for the problems he outlines. His final work should be praised as a diagnostic look at an America in desperate need of a cure, which Lasch had not found at the time of his death.

The Politics of the Christian Right

Daniel J. Jones

Michael Lienesch: **Redeeming America: Piety and Politics in the New Christian Right.** Chapel Hill: University of North Carolina Press, 1993. 332 pp. $45.00.

Michael Lienesch attempts to make sense of the political activities of conservative Christians in his book *Redeeming America: Piety and Politics in the New Christian Right*. In chapters entitled "Self," "Family," "Polity," and "World," Lienesch draws heavily on works by New Christian Right (NCR) leaders such as Pat Robertson, Jerry Falwell, Phyllis Schlafly, and Anita Bryant to explain the past failures of the religious conservative movement while looking ahead toward its probable future.

Lienesch makes the argument that the NCR is not a movement peculiar to the 1980s; it is an extension of a movement that has been in existence since the early nineteenth century. Believing that its return is all but inevitable in the 1990s, Lienesch writes: "The Christian right is less like a star than a comet that appears and retreats along a more-or-less regular path, attracting our attention periodically and then seeming to disappear, retreating but always returning."

From recent works by NCR leaders, it seems that there are two basic perspectives on why the Christian right lost its influence and credibility in the late 1980s. One camp, Lienesch says, contends that the failures of the Christian right can be attributed to its abstract idealism and its "triumphalist" mentality. By holding idealistic but militantly stated goals, Lienesch believes, the Christian right lost the respect of many of its potential followers. Regarding its "triumphalist" mentality, Lienesch asserts that the movement overestimated its successes by claiming responsibility for the election of Reagan and other conservatives throughout the country. Lienesch cites a number of sources concluding that the Christian right wanted to "announce the score when the team won and change the conversation when the team lost." This camp, says Lienesch, saw the Christian right at its strongest when it "went with the flow" and concentrated upon clearly defined issues and goals, such as opposition to the Equal Rights Amendment and various gay rights bills.

Conversely, the second camp avers that the Christian right was at its worst when it "went with the flow." Proponents of this view believe that the Christian right succumbed to mainstream ideals and thereby lost the respect of its most engaged followers. With this in mind, Lienesch argues that the New Christian right's problems can be traced to its lack of direction and group cohesion. He writes of how "the willingness of the new Christian right to play by the pluralist rules of the political system-led religious conservatives into ill-advised alliances with those who were its enemies rather than its friends."

Unfortunately, Lienesch loses his own voice in the discussion of the failings of the Christian right in the 1980s. He unsuccessfully attempts to incorporate a plethora of possible views to explain the waning of the NCR while never coming to a conclusion himself. Whether intentionally or not, Lienesch leaves it up to the reader to decide which views are the most plausible as to why the Christian right lost the respect of its followers.

Drawing from both perspectives on the failure of Christian conservatism in the 1980s, Lienesch discusses its possible future. Here he seems more sure of himself and his opinions. With respect to the current momentum of the movement, he writes: "The Christian right at the beginning of the 1990s can best be seen as a movement in which categories are collapsing and traditional political and theological boundaries are becoming blurred." From his understanding, the NCR has decided to work within the present political situation, to "go with the flow," only this time concentrating on the state and local levels of government.

Lienesch assserts that the NCR will become less and less prominent in national politics, while becoming more and more visible locally. He believes that, to regain respect, the movement will have to become more cohesive: "Having learned from hard experience to eschew broad based and highly ideological strategies they will probably focus upon specific issues like abortion." Here again, however, Lienesch tends to be suspicious of his own conclusions.

In the end, all he seems to be sure of is that the NCR needs to seek long-term strategies which involve "political participation at its most fundamental level"—which is state and local government.

Throughout the book Lienesch appears less like a partisan than an interested student. He extracts a number of different views from religious conservative leaders, yet he never comes to a satisfactory conclusion as to which one is most credible. He offers some insights on where the Christian conservative movement is going but has less to say on where it has been. Instead, Lienesch presents an informative collection of opinions about why the strength of the Christian right waxes and wanes. *Redeeming America: Piety and Politics in the New Christian Right* can only be recommended to novice readers looking to pick up a bit of understanding about the New Christian Right today. What they will acquire are the opinions of commentators and a smattering of factual information.

Class, Inherited Intelligence, and the Quality of Leadership

Alan J. Levine

Richard Herrnstein and Charles Murray: **The Bell Curve: Intelligence and Class Structure in American Life.** New York: Free Press, 1994. 845 pp. $30.00.

The Bell Curve has already become a classic *succès de scandale,* a best-seller that has drawn violent censure. Few recent books have evoked so many temper tantrums disguised as book reviews. Curiously, this reaction has not been caused by its main thesis, but by one aspect of a relatively subsidiary issue, an argument that the authors advance only tentatively, viz., that black Americans, on average, are inferior to whites in intelligence, and largely for genetic reasons. The main argument of *The Bell Curve* and other aspects of the book that might be expected to upset many people have caused little comment; but the authors' remarks on race and intelligence have obviously hit a nerve in our race-obsessed society.

Those who feel compelled to pretend that we have already heard the last word on race, sexuality, and the differences between the sexes find this book hard to stomach; such dyspeptic readers have clearly become more sensitive lately. It is interesting to note the contrast between the reception given *The Bell Curve* and the treatment afforded John R. Baker's cleverly argued and sinister book *Race,* published by Oxford University Press twenty years earlier. Although the latter, the work of a distinguished biologist, was issued by one of the most prestigious university presses in the world, and was far more objectionable than *The Bell Curve,* it attracted much less attention. It received some violently hostile reviews, but sank like a stone. Conversely, the most bitter critics of *The Bell Curve* have acted as though they felt compelled to publicize it because of the race issue. But the central argument of the book has little to do with race, and it can stand or fall without reference to the racial issue. Indeed, *The Bell Curve* is an interesting, informative, and useful work even though its main argument, as well as the racial one, seems to me to be very dubious.

The main thesis of *The Bell Curve* is an elaboration of an old notion: American society, like Western society in general, is to an increasing extent a meritocracy, run by the most capable and intelligent without regard to their social origin. In the first half of the twentieth century, only a comparatively small portion of the population received a college or even a secondary education. And the minority in college was not even the smartest part of the upper social class. As late as 1950, most business executives had been born into well-off WASP families. However, intelligent people, that is, those who had high intelligence quotients, were widely spread through all sectors of society and all income levels, just as they had been in all other societies throughout history. Intelligence was not concentrated in any particular class.

Since then, the authors maintain, our society has undergone a revolution few have appreciated, or even recognized. The removal of barriers to various ethnic and religious groups, the immense growth of secondary and higher education, the wide availability of scholarships, and the widening of recruitment in business have established an unprecedented trend. People of high intelligence, regardless of the social and economic status wherein they were born, are being selected for and concentrated in the upper stratum of society. They form a "cognitive elite." (This elite, however, is increasingly isolated socially, and even physically, from the rest of the population, and in some ways is rather ignorant.) Intelligence is converging with affluence, at the top. Meanwhile, the real income of blue-collar workers (as opposed to white-collar workers) has become static. The lower stratum of society, increasingly drained of intelligent members by the sorting process, finds it harder and harder to get along in a job marker that increasingly rewards intelligence, not just education. And the lower class is undermined by the effects of the sexual revolution and its supposed concomitant, the growing dissolution of marriage, drugs, and welfare policies. Working families face the threat of being swallowed up by the underclass, which is more or less unemployed (and often unemployable) and characterized by broken or never-formed families, illegitimacy, crime, and drug addiction. Children born in that group, whatever their potential (which probably isn't much) have little chance of success. Their parents, if any are around, have poor parenting skills, when they are not downright abusive, and cannot properly socialize children. The underclass has already largely gobbled up the less well-off part of the black population, and is threatening to overwhelm lower-class whites as well. The illegitimacy rate, which the authors take as a key indicator of social disintegration, has already reached 22 percent among American whites. The authors believe that once the black illegitimacy rate reached 25 percent, it and other measures of undesirable behaviors entered an explosive stage which will probably have repercussions among whites. (It is interesting to note that this important prediction, probably the most chilling in *The Bell Curve,* seems to have attracted no attention at all.)

Moreover, legitimately or not, the "cognitive elite" is not reproducing itself as fast as the lower and less intelligent groups. The underclass, especially, is enabled, if not encouraged, to have children by welfare policies. The situation is complicated by the addition of immigrants, who, although not prone to underclass-type behavior (at least the first generation) are, mostly, less gifted than their predecessors and native-born whites, and whose arrival may involve considerable direct and immediate costs to society.

These "dysgenic pressures" matter especially (although not only) because the authors believe that intelligence is largely determined by heredity. The authors cite estimates of the heritability of intelligence ranging from a minimum of 40 to a maximum of 80 percent, but seem inclined to believe the higher figures. And Herrnstein and Murray seem to think that our society has *already* been largely "sorted out." There are relatively few good genes remaining outside the "cognitive elite." At least among whites, there is no longer a significant number of talented youths denied educational opportunity because of economic disadvantage. As people of less intelligence reproduce themselves, or enter the country, and the "cognitive elite" fails to reproduce itself at a comparable rate, America is being permanently dumbed down. And, insofar as intelligence my be environmentally determined, that is little cause for comfort, for it is hard to manipulate the environment so as to improve intelligence. Intelligence quotients are largely settled and stable by the time a child goes to school. Attempts to boost intelligence by "early intervention"—

Head Start and its many rivals—have generally failed; apparent early gains seem to disappear later. The prospects of improving education, in any case, are not good. "Powerful teachers' organizations will not tolerate certification tests that flunk large numbers of teachers. Organizations that represent minority groups will not tolerate national educational standards that cause large numbers of minority children to flunk."

American society is thus well underway to forming a castelike structure, with an increasingly isolated and outnumbered upper class at the top, and a growing disorderly, vicious, and stupid lower class, ridden by bitter clashes between ethnic groups. The authors expect an eventual shift from a welfare state to a "custodial state" characterized by a "Latin American" style of conservationism rather than the traditional Anglo-American brand, bluntly aimed at holding down the have-nots, and possibly characterized by an explosive growth of racial prejudice. For blacks, and to a lesser extent Latinos, will remain disproportionately on the bottom.

It is the comparatively subsidiary ethnic aspects of this unpleasant vision that have attracted the most attention. The authors stress that ethnic groups differ in average intelligence, as measured in IQ tests. Blacks, on average, are less intelligent than Latinos, who in turn are less intelligent than non-Hispanic whites. The latter lag behind East Asians, whose average IQ may be as much as ten points higher, although at a lesser distance than separates whites (average IQ 100) from blacks (average IQ 85.) The authors note, in passing, that Jews seem to have the highest scores of all. (Strangely, or perhaps not so strangely, the authors fail to note that Scandinavians also outperform other whites on intelligence tests.) Their reporting of the well-known differences between black and white average IQs, their arguments that the tests are fair, their estimate that intelligence is largely hereditary, and their conclusion that there are probably substantial innate differences between groups have attracted the most attention and provoked the most hostility.

It is a most curious fact, though one not much noticed, that *The Bell Curve*'s acceptance of the superiority of East Asians has caused little protest. Do present-day whites have so little self-respect that such ideas do not bother them? Or have they been so indoctrinated in group self-abnegation that they are unwilling to express resentment at such claims? Or are some whites so intent on "getting" blacks that they are willing to swallow such unpleasantness as long as the wretched blacks are put in their place?

In fact, too much has been made of the authors' arguments about heredity and racial differences, which are often quite cautious and qualified. They readily concede, whenever necessary, that the facts do not mesh, and they do present alternatives to their favored argument. Above all, they reject drawing any drastic policy recommendations from their arguments. They remind the reader that group averages are one thing, individuals another. Their conclusion, they believe, would demand the elimination of affirmative action, but they think that the proper alternative to present policies of racial favoritism is equal opportunity, not a different pattern of discrimination. To be sure, their caution is more than justified.

Herrnstein and Murray are quite successful (like some of their predecessors) in knocking down some of the more drastic attacks on the validity of intelligence tests. It is not true that "IQ tests measure only performance on IQ tests"; nor are the tests culturally biased. No one has been able to prove such biases; nor would such biases explain why Asians do better than whites on tests devised by member of the latter group, or why Amerinds, farther removed from the American cultural mainstream than blacks, outperform the latter. Although IQ tests may not reliably measure "pure" or "innate" or "potential" intelligence, however that may be defined, the results of such tests correlate fairly well with success in school and later life. They do test effective or operational intelligence.

The questions are whether there is a one-to-one relationship between the latter and innate potential, and to what extent the latter is hereditary. The range of estimates for the heritability of intelligence suggests unreliability. The high estimate, that intelligence is 80 percent hereditary, seems to be based on studies of separated identical twins. Historically, such studies have not proven reliable. And they have always tended to overstate heritability, for the separated twins are almost never placed in very different environments. There is good reason to doubt that IQ is a stable hereditary characteristic. Herrnstein and Murray themselves note that the gap between black and white IQs has narrowed by three points in a generation. It is worth noting, in this connection, that the average IQ of the Japanese have risen seven points since World War II. Although adopted children generally do not resemble their adoptive parents in IQ, Herrnstein and Murray note that the IQs of adoptees from the lower class, placed in middle-class homes, leap six points ahead of those of their natural parents. Herrnstein and Murray properly cite this as a strong argument in favor of encouraging adoptions, including trans-racial adoptions, which current policies often discourage or forbid. (Some studies, which they do not mention, point to even more drastic increases of IQ in adopted children, of up to 20 points.) And, while Head Start and other early intervention programs aimed at young children may not have had a permanent useful effect—although other, cautious observers are not quite as pessimistic about them as Herrnstein and Murray—one must wonder why, if intelligence is substantially hereditary, such programs should have any effect at all. Herrnstein and Murray seem reluctant to explore the problems of intelligence at the other end of the scale where geniuses rarely transmit their qualities to their offspring. The obscurities of intelligence are suggested by the well-established effect that twins have an average IQ five points below that of their non-twin siblings.

There are alternatives to the bare choice between the propositions "the tests are biased" and "IQ tests prove that blacks are inherently less intelligent." Herrnstein and Murray themselves note the arguments advance by Jane Mercer and John Ogbu, who suggest that the poor performances of blacks on IQ tests may be due to diffuse cultural effects perhaps connected with the castelike position they had occupied in American society until recently. The authors knock down part of Mercer's attempt to prove her case, but do not completely refute it. Indeed, Mercer's and Ogbu's arguments may make more sense if inverted. It is rather noticeable that the groups Herrnstein and Murray cite as having high IQs—e.g., Ashkenazic Jews, Japanese, and Chinese—have, broadly speaking, been civilized longer than most white Europeans who, in turn, have been civilized longer than sub-Saharan Africans. Hereditarians might argue that the people first civilized had higher intelligence to begin with. But perhaps having been civilized for a long time produces subtle changes that encourage greater effectiveness at turning "potential" into "effective" intelligence. Such arguments aside, it seems absurd to assume that group historical or family traditions have no important effect on how children's minds develop. What could be sillier than assuming that Jews—whose ancestors have been literate towndwellers for many centuries, and the descendants of slaves, who were hewers of wood and drawers of water—would *not* influence their children's upbringing in differing directions? We may not be able to measure the differences involved, but it is unlikely that they do not exist. But many believers in environmental explanations, not just hereditarians, seem reluctant to explore such issues.

In any case, the history of gross misinterpretations of data and the frequent sloppiness of the relevant studies (especially, but not only, of twins) that have characterized the study of both intelligence and racial differences, the danger of mistaking correlations for causes, the difficulty of threading one's way through the maze of possible environmental factors, and the existence of facts that cannot be fitted into *either* hereditarian or environmental explanations call for extreme caution in such matters, more extreme than Herrnstein and Murray display.

The stress that the authors place on the probable explosive growth of a white underclass, remarks like "it matters little whether the genes are involved at all" in ethnic differences, and their pointed comment "If women with low (IQ) scores are reproducing more rapidly than women with high scores, the distribution of scores will, other things being equal, decline no matter whether the women with low scores came by them through nature or nurture," make it hard to understand why they bothered to enter controversies over heredity and racial differences. That may have been Richard Herrnstein's hobbyhorse, rather than Charles Murray's. Indeed, although few seem to have noticed it, *The Bell Curve*'s stress on heredity, and other generally intractable and long-range causes of social problems, is quite different from the thrust of *Losing Ground,* the work that made Charles Murray famous. In that book, Murray tried to show that modest changes in government policies had rapid and disastrous consequences.

Some of those policies, as described in both *Losing Ground* and *The Bell Curve,* and a look at contemporary society in general, suggest that there is something seriously wrong with the core thesis of the latter book, something that even (or especially) the bitterest critics have been unwilling to explore, perhaps because the implications of such an exploration may seem decidedly "reactionary." This reviewer and his family (like Herrnstein and Murray) have benefited from many of the moves toward meritocracy that the authors of *The Bell Curve* celebrate, even as they deplore some of their consequences. I am decidedly uneasy with some of what I have to say; nevertheless, someone should say it.

Even the critics of *The Bell Curve* seem to accept the thesis that America is a meritocracy, except perhaps for certain racial minorities, or at least has become relatively more meritocratic than it was in 1900. Brains, from a wider variety of backgrounds, do get to the top more often now than then. And it is true that both the vast variety of statistics offered by Herrnstein and Murray and most people's experience confirm both the existence of the sorting process and of greater fairness today. But the "proof of the pudding is in the eating," and when one asks whether the "cognitive elite" is managing society more effectively, or even more humanely, than its less intelligent predecessors—whether its intelligence has done it and the rest of us much good—the answer is not too reassuring. Curiously, even Herrnstein and Murray seem to express some doubts about the "cognitive elite," remarking "Whether one looks at the worlds of science, literature, politics or the arts, one does not get the impression that the top of the IQ distribution is filled with more subtle, insightful or powerful intellects than it was in our grandparent's day."

A comparison between the "cognitive elite" and its predecessors, of a somewhat different sort than that in *The Bell Curve,* may be interesting. It is probable, in the first place, that Herrnstein and Murray have exaggerated the contrast between the two a bit; the United States in the early twentieth century was already more "meritocratic" than they allow, and it is likely that the shift to more open business recruitment, noted by W. Lloyd Warner, was underway earlier than they suppose. But it is probably true to say that in 1900 the United States was run largely by men who got "gentleman Cs" at Harvard or Yale, or people of the same sort who never attended any college. They had their unattractive side. Some of them were greedy, callous, and snobbish toward those whom they regarded as their social inferiors. In accordance with present-day obsessions with ethnicity, Herrnstein and Murray perhaps overplay the extent to which they were prejudiced in such matters, while overlooking the role of sheer class prejudice. Up to the New Deal, they often treated workers, whatever the latter's ethnicity, very badly indeed. They were sometimes stupid, and were capable of gross blunders, for example, stumbling into the Great Depression. Still, they were rarely deliberately inhumane, and the United States prospered and advanced under their domination. They many have made mistakes, and sometimes behaved badly, though less so than any other dominant group in history, but their policies were not insane.

This is more than can be said of quite a few of the policies pursued by their successors. Many of these policies, some bitterly documented in *The Bell Curve,* contradict the very basis of the "cognitive elite" itself. What is one to think of an elite, based on intelligence and education, which has dumbly accepted the Supreme Court's forbidding employers from using intelligence tests, although the latter are of proven worth in employment? This "elite" has concentrated an overwhelming proportion of aid to education on attempts (not too successful) to help the least gifted students as Herrnstein and Murray show, while less than one tenth of one percent of federal aid to education goes to helping gifted students. This and the "elite" has allowed its own education to deteriorate and is almost the sole prop of affirmative action. It has allowed a few bigots to discourage, even forbid, trans-racial adoptions. Unlike its Japanese counterpart, it is hardly even reproducing itself. If we broaden our view to other matters, we find the "cognitive elite" pursuing, often with amazingly obstinacy, policies long since proved insane, or obviously insane to begin with. It has tolerated, if not encouraged, a rise in crime unthinkable early in this century; a substantial element of it continues to obstruct any attempt to deal with this problem. It has based our social welfare and immigration policies on antithetical assumptions, and has gone on to policies of multiculturalism and bilingualism that discard all the things that make it possible for the United States to weld together people of different origins. It is probably the first group in history to think that you can pull people together by constantly harping on their differences and grievances. For all of its addiction to "progressive" posturing, it has managed to revive many traditional evils. Let us note one of its most historic achievements; turning the mentally ill into the streets and resurrecting mass homelessness, one of the worst features of the Great Depression, in a period of prosperity and costly social programs. It has failed to oppose, and has probably promoted, the disintegration of the lowest class of the population, a phenomena for which it is hard to find much precedent.

This "cognitive elite" may be intelligent, but the more important fact about it is the lunacy of its rule.

Defending Public Morality

Anthony M. Matteo

Robert P. George: **Making Men Moral.** Oxford: Clarendon Press, 1993. 241 pp.

Does the state have any role in making men moral? Can it effectively legislate morality? If one is talking about behavior in the public domain encompassing acts such as murder, robbery, rape, or embezzlement, then there is little dispute. The state's primary obligation is to uphold "public morality": through legislation and punishment it ought to protect innocent citizens against the rapacious tendencies of those inclined to criminality. But if the behavior in question falls within the private domain—involving so-called "victimless crimes" such as pornography, prostitution, drug use, or homosexual sodomy—then one finds a fearsome contemporary debate. In *Making Men Moral* Robert P. George enters the fray on the side of what he calls the "central tradition" rooted in Aristotle and Thomas Aquinas. At the heart of this tradition is the belief that "sound politics and good law *are* concerned with helping people to lead morally upright and valuable lives, and, indeed, that a good political society may provide people with some protection from the corrupting influences of vice" (20).

In chapter 1 George surveys the philosophical underpinnings of this moral/legal tradition. Aristotle rejected the Sophist notion that law is merely a "guarantor of mens' rights against one another" in favor of a view that envisioned the law as a central shaping force leading the citizens of the *polis (polity)* to *eudaimonia* (well-being). The role of any genuine political community, then, goes beyond merely protecting the person and property of citizens against attack; it also includes the formidable duty of creating a societal environment that conduces to making men moral. For Aristotle, a moral life was one in which reason governed passion and emotion. People must be educated from their earliest years to develop a character sturdy enough to effect such rational control over the powerful lure of subrational impulses. Indeed, except for the elite few endowed by nature with a sufficiently virtuous character adequate to this task, the masses of men would fail at leading moral lives without the coercive power of law keeping their passions in check.

Aquinas follows Aristotle's lead on this score, but has a healthy sense of the law's limits in curbing all vice. In his words: "The purpose of law is to lead men to virtue, not suddenly, but gradually. Therefore it does not lay upon the multitude of imperfect men the burdens of those who are already virtuous, viz., that they should abstain from all evil" (*Summa Theologiae*, I-II, q. 95, a. 1.). As George points out, Aquinas' caveat as to the extent of morals legislation is rooted in prudence, not (as many contemporaries would contend) in some moral right to privacy that carries with it a moral right to do wrong. "[Aquinas]...judges it morally right to refrain from legally prohibiting vice where, given the condition of the people, the prohibition is likely to be futile or, worse yet, productive of more serious vices or wrongs" (32). So one might oppose rigorous enforcement of, say, laws prohibiting sodomy—without first committing oneself to the moral neutrality or even rectitude of the act—because such enforcement is impractical or would require tyrannical measures to be successful. As George rightly observes, neither Aristotle nor Aquinas assert that simply obeying laws restricting vice represents a sufficient condition of a truly moral life. Laws can only command external conformity to right standards of behavior, not the free internal conformity that is the essence of the moral life. But laws can play a subsidiary role in making us moral by inducing us away from vice when we are tempted and by promoting an overall healthy moral environment in which to live.

In chapters 2 through 6 of this work George seeks to defend this central tradition by dissecting the arguments of some of its most distinguished contemporary critics. In chapter 2 George reconsiders the famous debate between Patrick Devlin and H. L. A. Hart precipitated by the Wolfenden Report (September, 1957), which recommended to the British Parliament that homosexual behavior between consenting adults be decriminalized. Although George supports Devlin's conclusion (contra Hart) that the legal enforcement of morals can be justified, he calls into question the cogency of Devlin's supporting argumentation. Unlike the Aristotelian-Thomistic tradition, Devlin propounds a "noncognitivist" moral epistemology: moral beliefs are grounded in "feeling," not reason, and are historically inextricably intertwined with one or another religious tradition. Despite this "emotivist" and ultimately "relativist" view of ethics, Devlin, nonetheless, supports the legal enforcement of morals to protect the social cohesion of the community. "He claimed that society is justified in enforcing a societal morality as a means of self-preservation" (51). The tradition defended by George sees the matter quite differently. Its "realist" moral vision commits it to the capacity of reason to make objective judgements about what is *truly* right and wrong. Moral claims must be rationally defensible, and their validity does not hinge ultimately on individual or collective feeling or sentiment. This tradition asserts that the "truth" of the moral obligation or moral prohibition in question is a necessary condition for justified morals legislation. Hence, social cohesion rooted in an untrue morality is not a good in the eyes of this tradition. In fact, human well-being might be better served if highly cohesive societies organized around fallacious moral norms (say, Nazism or Stalinism) disintegrate. At any rate, it would seem that only a brand of moral realism, akin to the tradition George is supporting, can engage in intrasocietal and intersocietal moral critique in a principled fashion.

In chapters 3 through 6 George engages in a similar critical dialogue with other leading ethical theorists who oppose one or another tenet of the Aristotelian/Thomist moral tradition. Space does not permit me a full rendering of the fruitful insights that a close reading of this section might yield. However, I would like to mention some of the salient points that George propounds. He effectively shows that Ronald Dworkin's conception of individual "rights" reduces to an assertion of the inviolable nature of personal preferences. Thus, Dworkin must defend a view of privacy that forces government to respect the "equality" of its citizens by not favoring the preferences of one group over another. Contrary to the tradition, the state must not be in the business of favoring one view of the good life over another. But, as George asserts, "the natural law theory of individual rights and collective interests has the advantage over anti-perfectionist liberalism of providing a rational account of the moral foundations of rights by understanding them as implication of intrinsic human goods" [93]. From the point of view of the tradition, something is not "good" because people desire it, but people ought to desire what is objectively "good": that is, that which can be shown by rational analysis to promote human well being. One could only claim a right to that which can be shown to be a necessary condition of human flourishing. From this perspective it is hard to see how the desire for drugs, pornography, and liaisons with prostitutes need be elevated to the status of individual rights which the government must respect. Thus, morals laws that seek to protect and promote objective human flourishing need not violate anyone's properly conceived individual rights.

George is particularly masterful in his dissection of John Rawls's attack on morals legislation based on his famed decision-making process from behind the "veil of ignorance." According to Rawls, in the "original position" behind the veil rational individuals, ignorant of what their preferences might actually be in the society they are constructing, would opt for government neutrality toward opposing preferences as a matter of basic self-interest. Not knowing whether one might in fact be enamored of pornography, prostitution, or homosexuality, one would rationally oppose morals legislation directed against these practices in the original position. But as George astutely comments: "Rational people in the real world care about their beliefs not because their beliefs are *theirs,* but rather because their beliefs are (they suppose) *true*; rational people care about the ultimate ends...they have chosen to pursue, not because their ends are *theirs,* but because their ends are (they suppose) *worthy*" (134). In other words, in actual practice those concerned about making truly "moral" decisions presuppose (albeit often unreflectively) a moral realism that holds that there is a moral truth to be preferred beyond the mere satisfaction of individual desires. And, thus, "[t]he practical reasoning of parties in the original position turns out to be distinctively anti-perfectionist liberal practical reasoning: practical reasoning which treats wants as reasons. The 'persons' in the original position are persons precisely as they are conceived by anti-perfectionist liberalism" (137).

So Rawls's purportedly "neutral" opposition to morals legislation turns out to be not so neutral after all. His creators of the just society smuggle an anti-realist moral epistemology behind the veil of ignorance which rules out *ab initio* the tradition's defense of morals legislation based on moral realism. George effectively unmasks the "original position" as a theoretical ruse that commits the fundamental fallacy of begging the question.

In his final chapter George offers what he admits is merely a sketch of a pluralistic perfectionist theory of civil liberties: an updated version of the tradition he defends with appropriate modifications for modern times. This requires, he argues, giving more attention than was the case with Aristotle and Aquinas to the "fact that diversity, liberty, and privacy are themselves important components of a decent social milieu and conditions for the attainment of many basic human goods" (190). As the quotation indicates, unlike many contemporary pundits, George does not fall into the trap of promoting them as intrinsic goods. They are purely of instrumental value and can be abused as well as used for constructive ends. But this still leaves us with the perplexing practical question: when and how ought government to intervene to curtail immoral behavior of the sort at which morals legislation is directed? Mindful of Aquinas's counsel in this area, George responds that "the question of enforcing specific moral obligations is fundamentally a matter of prudence and will thus pivot on knowledge of circumstances that are necessarily local and contingent" (190). I take this to mean that George has a robust sense that providing a theoretical defense of morals laws is one thing; practically implementing them in ways that bring about more harm than good is another. The failure of Prohibition and the current fiasco that is labeled the War on Drugs should sound a loud and clear cautionary note to those who wish to rush headlong from theory to practice in this area.

George has done an admirable job of elucidating and defending the theoretical basis of laws directed to making men moral. What we need now is some practical guide to overcoming the seemingly intractable problems implementing such laws present. Perhaps, in the end, we might discover that in most instances "persuasion" rather than "coercion" is the best strategy. A local boycott of stores that traffic in pornography seems like a far less perilous path than the appointment of government censors and granting expanded powers to police vice squads.

Defending Science

Alan J. Levine

Paul R. Gross and Norman Levitt: **Higher Superstition: The Academic Left and Its Quarrels With Science.** Baltimore, Md.: Johns Hopkins University Press, 1994. 314 pp.

A notable feature of contemporary Western—and especially American—culture is its hostility to the scientific enterprise necessary to its existence. The enmity of popular culture toward science and scientists is familiar to every TV viewer and has been well documented by Stanley Rothman. But there has been a notable reluctance to analyze the even more vehement, and probably more dangerous, hostility toward science among the (supposedly) highly educated. Academic leftists, the "PC crowd," openly dislike science, a fact that should tell us a lot about them. Paul Gross, a biologist, and Norman Levitt, a mathematician, have written a very effective study of an increasingly dangerous social trend. *Higher Superstition* is notable for its clarity of analysis, especially in dealing with the misdeeds of apocalyptic ecological fanatics, feminist extremists, and ethnic tribalists, all of whom have wither attacked science outright, or have done their best to warp it into the service of some particular ideological fanaticism. Gross and Levitt expose such muddled thinking. Although their book is hardly pleasant reading, it is leavened with a welcome sense of humor as it recounts the antics of people totally lacking that quality. The characters with whom the authors deal are remarkable for their arrogance, ignorance, addiction to moral one-upmanship, and diffuse accusations against other people. When Gross and Levitt's targets deign to actually deal with the work of scientists, the results are often pompous fakery, based on gross misreading of the sources.

At the bottom of this stance, Gross and Levitt emphasize, lies more than either any traditional hostility of humanists and social scientists toward the "hard" sciences or the chagrin of social scientists at the failure of their crude efforts to imitate the methods of natural scientists. Although such resentments are significant, the main element of the left's attitude is anger at the failure of the world to conform to its desires and distorted image of reality. The result has been an intensified hatred of Western civilization and its vital features, of which science is perhaps the foremost and the greatest source of Western power. "No other civilization has a like gem in its crown. Thus science becomes and irresistible target for those Western intellectuals whose sense of their own heritage has become an intolerable moral burden." Instead of being seen as a liberating force, science is interpreted as a handmaiden of capitalism, imperialism, sexism, and the other real and supposed evils of the Western world. The authors dryly note that the "history of Western artistic and intellectual achievement no longer provides hope or inspiration—on the contrary, it taunts and irritates." Hatred for the West, they note, is the central element; what at first sight might seem to be attraction to or interest in other cultures or ways of doing things is something else. New writers, artists, musicians, and philosophers are "put forward for what they are not—white, European, male." The obsessions that the academic left expresses in its assaults on science are authentic derivatives from the *zeitgeist* of the 1960s; above all, the authors note, the emergence of the idea of the "special competence" (it might be more accurate to say "special rights") of the oppressed or supposedly oppressed. Only blacks, Amerinds, Chicanos, women, homosexuals, and the like have the right to analyze, or even talk about, their respective groups. Conversely, a group traditionally privileged, or supposed to have been privileged, has no right to "define reality" for the supposed "victim" groups. And, proponents of these views believe, science and scientists, not nature, define reality. Indeed, it is really society as whole that does so. Science is merely a social product, a convention or discourse governed by social practices, not a uniquely effective and objective access to reality. This is meant quite literally. Stanley Aronowitz, a leading exponent of this school, holds that Einstein did not conceive of relativity in a disinterested quest for the nature of the universe, but as an instrument of late nineteenth-century capitalism and imperialism, because the advance of technology "needed" his ideas. (Of course, the application of his theories was totally unexpected and followed the publication of the Special Theory of Relativity by forty years.)

The central common feature of the maniacs whom Gross and Levitt analyze is "perspectivism." All the traditional ideas of Western civilization, including science, are merely "local truths," if not deliberately manufactured by the upholders of "hierarchy." Science is no more valid than, say, Melanesian witchcraft—or maybe less so if one needs the additional injunction that the previously "disempowered" must be specially recognized. Unfortunately, these ideas are common, even dominant, in academia, where the left dominates faculties and administrators pander to it. Leftist jackasses are well connected and enjoy an astonishingly free ride. Feminists, in particular, occupy a privileged place.

Gross and Levitt's critique is especially interesting, since, as they stress, they themselves are men of the left. They carefully distance themselves from other critics of academic life like Roger Kimball. Indeed, their posture of "gee whiz, fellas, we're really sympathetic left types too" sometimes becomes tiresome, as does their tendency to exaggerate the academic left's isolation from wider society. Discussing the nineteenth century and its ideas of progress, they grumble that the "industrialists' prosperity was the mill workers' hell," and that "the superiority of the technologized economic superstructure of Europe and the United States exacted a terrible tribute from millions of Chinese, Indians, Latin Americans and Filipinos, who had no reason to praise the scientific virtuosity that showered them with shells and bullets." Such concepts of the Industrial Revolution and nineteenth-century expansions are far from accurate. Gross and Levitt even beat their breasts about the extent to which women were once deliberately excluded from science. They overstress, in countering prevalent demonologies, the extent to which science was aligned with "progressive" or liberal ideas in the last century, and tend to carelessly assume that what they consider enlightened values were always deemed such. A good case can by made, I think, that "hard" scientists have always been fairly open-minded and humane, but it would be hard to show that, in the nineteenth century, they had much interest or belief in racial or sexual equality or a fair break for indigenous peoples. It is even less true that such values concerned social scientists. Sociology, it is well known, was invented by conservatives, while anthropologists, at least up to the 1890s, were thoroughly in favor of racial prejudice. To be sure, the politically correct view of science in general as merely a tool of late Victorian hierarchy is even less well founded. By 1900, the Jews, until recently an outcast group in most Western countries, were beginning to contribute a very disproportionate number of scientists, and a few non-Western scientists, especially Indians and Japanese, were beginning to appear. Anyhow, non-Western societies have amply showed that mystical justifications for hierarchy have been far more effective than anything perpetrated by scientists. Indian caste is a case in point.

Gross and Levitt closely analyze the subtypes of the attack on science. For extreme feminists, science is a male enterprise biased by the values of our male-dominated society (as though anyone had found any society anywhere that is not male dominated). For the "apocalyptic naturist," science is to blame for the environmental crisis, which is also the latest final crisis of capitalism (now that one doesn't have imperialism to kick around anymore). A movement called "ecofeminism" aims to accommodate feminists with a penchant for environmental activism. The danger, Gross and Levitt rightly stress, is that political extremism of this sort will either discredit, or cause the misdirection of, responses to the real environmental dangers that do exist. Although environmentalism, more than any other political cause that has ever existed, owes everything to science, a large number of ecofreaks have attacked science for "desanctifying nature" and lending itself to the alleged predations of industrial society. Critics of science prefer neopagan personifications or the anthropomorphosizing of nature (which entails the dehumanization of human beings) and hysterical fears of "retribution" from nature. For them, everything artificial or manmade is bad, while natural products—presumably including tobacco, cobra venom, and bubonic plague germs—are good. A somewhat parallel turn against scientific modes of understanding has taken place among AIDS activists. Gross and Levitt analyze this with some care, despite their obvious anxiety about offending homosexual activists.

Perhaps worst of all, however, are the fruits of ethnic and sexual tribalism, most prominently represented by "Afrocentrism." Tribalist activists seem to have struck at a central social weakness. Gross and Levitt grimly conclude that "tribalism, in one form or another, is the most favored project of leftist ideologues, who appear to have abandoned, for the moment, the universalism, that once shone through even the dreariest left-wing cant." Afrocentrism, with its "flagrant falsification," is perhaps the biggest danger of all. At stake, the authors suggest, is not the fate of science as such—there is no reason for scientists to be acutely alarmed in the short run—but the ability of our culture as a whole to use and evaluate science intelligently. "To the extent that the academic left's critique becomes the dominant mode of thinking about science on the part of non-scientists, that thinking will be distorted and dangerously irrelevant." Some fields, notably anthropology, have already fallen victim to "antiscientific relativism."

Contributors

ARYEH BOTWINICK is professor of philosophy at Temple University and the author of several books on postmodernist social and epistemological criticism, including *Postmodernism and Democratic Theory* (Temple University Press, 1993).

ROBERT BRESLER is Dean of the Social Sciences at Pennsylvania State University (Harrisburg). He has authored a widely used textbook on U.S. government and is currently working on a study of cold war liberalism.

HANS-HERMANN HOPPE is professor of economics at the University of Nevada (Las Vegas), and has published books and essays on Austrian economics.

ANTHONY M. MATTEO is associate professor of philosophy at Elizabetown College and the author of *The Quest for the Absolute* (Northern Illinois University Press, 1992) and of numerous essays on ethical questions.

CHRIS WOLTERMANN holds a doctorate in political science from Purdue University and writes frequently for *Telos* and other periodicals on nationhood and national identity.

BOOKSHELF CONTRIBUTORS

ALAN J. LEVINE, a historian and free-lance writer residing in New York, has recently published *The Missile and Space Race,* his third book in three years, all with Praeger.

DANIEL JONES, JEREMY PIZZOLA, and **MELANIE REISER** are students in good standing in Professor Gottfried's courses in political theory.